BREATHING TECHNIQUE

POEMS BY
Marija Knežević

TRANSLATED FROM
THE SERBIAN BY
Sibelan Forrester

Zephyr Press | Brookline, Mass.

Printed in Michigan by Cushing Malloy, Inc.

Zephyr Press acknowledges with gratitude the financial
support of the Massachusetts Cultural Council
and the National Endowment for the Arts.

Zephyr Press, a non-profit arts and education 501(c)(3) organization,
publishes literary titles that foster a deeper understanding of cultures
and languages. Zephyr Press books are distributed to the trade in the U.S.
and Canada by Consortium Book Sales and Distribution [www.cbsd.com].

Cataloguing-in publication data is available from the Library of Congress.

ISBN 978-1-938890-81-9

ZEPHYR PRESS
www.zephyrpress.org

TABLE OF CONTENTS

A TECHNIQUE FOR EVERYTHING:
THE POET MARIJA KNEŽEVIĆ

Introduction by Sibelan Forrester

Marija Knežević's poetry has a particularly important quality: it rewards repeated reading. The first pass through gives enjoyment, certainly, but the pleasure of uncovering rich, deeper layers of meaning lies ahead.

Knežević was born in Belgrade in 1963 and grew up in that beautiful capital city on the Danube. She received her bachelor's degree from the University of Belgrade, specializing in Comparative Literature (known as "General Literature") and in Literary Theory. Some years later she earned a Master's degree in Comparative Literature at Michigan State University; during her graduate studies there she taught creative writing, among other things. She now lives once again in Belgrade, working as an independent editor, writer and translator.

Befitting a background in Comparative Literature, her work often refers to other works, though never so much that a reader who doesn't know the poets or singers or other sources cited will wind up high and dry. Some of her works have a "classical" feeling that recalls earlier eras in literature — for instance, "*Casa*," which celebrates an international poetic event and the sparks that struck poets from different countries; languages and traditions loosen up and party together. "The Apocalypse According to Orpheus" draws on a well-known classical story — one that lies at the origins of Western lyric poetry. Some of Knežević's poems rhyme, though that is rare; "My Neighborhood" attempts in translation to convey the rhyme scheme, though in a slantier manner. Some poems have what I can only call a magical quality, the visible traces of poetic inspiration — see the incantational quality in "The River's Name," excerpted from a longer poem. "*Fado Triste*" evokes the rhythm of that musical genre. Some poems have a markedly ironic twist, like "Holly Business," whose title (English in the original) puns on the similarity of 'holy' and 'holly[wood],' mocking the selfish desires of contemporary celebrities, not wholly without sympathy for their hunger for spiritual authenticity. The poem also comments on our era of glorifying "stars" (instead of artists, scientists . . .) and "reality" shows. Some of the poems present a little crystal of aphorism, as in "The Era of Tenderness," or a brief affectionate joke, like "Charlie." The currents of thought and inspiration can flow over historical tragedies and violence ("The Inca"), and sometimes very recent events. In "The Spirit from the Gas Bottle," for example, the translation includes a few exact quotes from *The Tempest*, but it mainly pertains to the tragic fates of more recent refugees sailing the Mediterranean — and to the moral obligations imposed on those who holiday along the same shores. Scholar and critic Zorica Bečanović Nikolić has described the poems as "Duboke [. . .] i vedre i gorke i ironične" (deep and cheerful and bitter and ironic): these are well-chosen words.

If several poems here bitterly describe the problems with contemporary society, recollections of past loves and pleasures nevertheless warm the city where those memories are set. Humor is a vital part of these poems, sometimes gentle and warm, other times with an edge or a bit of a grimace. Politics and human failings often feature in Marija Knežević's poetry, but her most essential topic is love.

I must say how great it has been to receive Marija's knowledgeable responses to my questions. I enjoyed the pleasure of working with a very gifted living poet alongside all the benefits of her superb knowledge of English. She is just as likely to refer to Auden, Plath or Shakespeare as to invoke Vesna Parun, Miodrag Pavlović or Izet Sarajlić, and she let me know what was most important to preserve in cases where (for instance) changing the original word order threatens major changes to the meaning. My first priority as a translator is to cling to the author's meaning, to represent the original as closely as I can. Of course music is a huge part of that meaning; a translator would struggle to reproduce the beauty of a phrase like "kroz prozor voza" ("through the train window," in *Fado Triste*), with its combination of vocal "Oh!" and buzzing (like an engine?) z's, but I strive to compensate in other places as English allows.

Marija herself recommended some of the poems that she felt were most representative. Although she assembles her books as coherent wholes that each tell a particular story, this edition was bound to be a selection from multiple volumes, including one not yet published. The rest of the poems in this volume I chose from broader reading among her works. A few poems I love would have required too many explanations to be enjoyable for a reader in English. Plenty more still await translation.

This poet packs a lot of meaning into her lines, and at times I had to do everything I could to compact the English, where articles and helping verbs pile up the obligatory syllables. (Even then, the first complete English draft had nearly 3000 more words than the Serbian originals!) It made my job easier that many of the poems call on contemporary Anglophone culture, with some episodes even set in the USA, where Knežević spent years of her life and where she has connections through family and friends. I also hope that the name of the real, not "reality," tennis star Martina Navrátilová will still be familiar to many readers.

ACKNOWLEDGMENTS

Warmest thanks to Zephyr Press and the paladins of poetry who work there: Jim Kates, Cris Mattison, and Leora Zeitlin. I owe huge gratitude to Marija herself: every single translation here has been blessed by her approval or improved by her careful reading and suggestions. She is almost as generous as she is talented! The librarians at Swarthmore College offered invaluable support for research of every kind, and research funding from Swarthmore allowed me to visit the poet in person in Belgrade. An earlier version of "The Spirit from the Gas Bottle" benefited from very helpful comments by Nathalie Anderson, Benjamin Ridgway, and Dima Hanna. Aleksandar Bošković offered me a chance to present some of my early work in progress to his students and colleagues at Columbia University. Special thanks and appreciation to the brilliant and tireless Dr. Svetlana Tomić, scholar and professor, who now lives and teaches in Belgrade. She first recommended that I read Marija Knežević's work, loaned me her own *signed* copies of two books, and then introduced me when she happened to see the poet across the street—definitely a sign that fate was intervening in my favor.

TEHNIKA DISANJA BREATHING TECHNIQUE

.

POČETAK KARTOGRAFIJE

Biti stvar
bez upotrebne vrednosti.
Biti stvar koja vremenom dobija na vrednosti
a niko ne zna zašto.
Dozvoliti da te nazivaju
ukrasnim predmetom.
Čuti da si višak.
Čuti da se bez tebe ne može.
Disati u sebi.
Menjati vlasnike.
Biti neposedovan.
Biti predmet divljenja.
Premeštati se,
izbeći seobe.
Biti dovoljan.

Biti brod.
Licem okrenut dnu biti
na oba kraja dubine.
Ostavljati trag
ne večan.
Uplovljavati.
Isplovljavati
na isti način.
Biti voljen u lukama.
Biti brod.
Voleti
veći deo života na otvorenom moru
sanjati o lukama.

THE BEGINNING OF CARTOGRAPHY

To be a thing
without use value.
To be a thing that gains value over time
though no one knows why.
To let yourself be called
a decorative item.
To hear that you're superfluous.
To hear they can't make it without you.
To breathe inside yourself.
To change owners.
To be unpossessed.
To be an object of admiration.
To change locations,
to avoid migration.
To be satisfied.

To be a ship.
Face turned to the sea floor to be
on both sides of the deep.
To leave a trace
not for eternity.
To sail in.
To sail out
the same way.
To be loved in harbors.
To be a ship.
To love
the better part of life in open sea
to dream of harbors.

Izbeći čekanje. Kretati se
uvek istom stazom
od luke ka njoj.
Zabavljen mrežama na palubi.
Pretvarati tovar u priče.
Biti brod.
Nositi sebe bez napora.

Biti rod. Svakome.
Muškarcima, ženama, algama,
tigrovima u skoku na jelena,
lotosima nastanjenim u sopstvenim suzama,
ostrvima, pećinama čija je bar jedna
odaja neispitana
biti orođen.

Voleti tebe
a to nikad ne saznati.
Biti uvek iznenada
nova radost i neočekivani bol.

Izbeći postojanje.
Kap
na tvojoj koži
koja je već sećanje na dodir.
Kap je već druga kap.

Biti zapravo nikad.
Biti sad.
Jednina u prolazu.

To avoid waiting. To move
always by the same path
from harbor back towards it.
Entranced by the nets on deck.
To transform cargo into stories.
To be a ship.
To bear yourself without effort.

To be kin. To anyone.
To men, women, algae,
tigers leaping at a deer,
lotuses settled in their own tears,
islands, caves who have at least one
chamber unexplored
to be related.

To love you
and never to learn it.
To be always suddenly
new joy and unexpected pain.

To avoid existence.
A drop
on your skin
that's already a memory of touch.
The drop's already another drop.

To be actually never.
To be now.
Singularity in passage.

POSLEDNJA LEKCIJA O NEŽNOSTI

Kad umrem,
obavezno ostavite prozor otvoren.
Hoću da nastavim da budem prizor
kroz koji sa tobom hodam
korak prirastao uz korak
kao neistražena životinjica
u šetnji
iz jedne u drugu vrstu.

I gramofom da ste mi uključili.
Ne volim tango sa traka,
još manje savršenstvo kompakt diskova.
Želim da na miru igram sa tobom
mislima
taj ples koji sam sa sobom pleše.
Nađite mi ploču koja pucketa.
Volim da volim u šumovima.

Otvorite mi sva tvoja pisma.
Žudim da ih njušim,
onako kako sam ih uvek čitala.

Na sto, kraj postelje
koja je uvek i samrtna,
stavite mi školjku i malu mirišljavu sveću.
Ako nađete miris vanile,
puno ste mi učinili.

THE LAST LECTURE ON TENDERNESS

When I die,
you must be sure to leave the window open.
I want to continue to be the spectacle
through which I walk with you
step grown into step
like an unresearched little animal
in a stroll
from one species into another.

And turn the record player on for me.
I don't like tango on tape,
still less the perfection of compact discs.
I want to dance with you in peace
by thoughts
the dance that dances with itself.
Find me a record that crackles.
I love to love in noises.

Open for me all your letters.
I'm greedy to sniff them
the same way I always read them.

On the table, beside the bed
that's always a deathbed too,
put a shell and a little scented candle.
If you find one the scent of vanilla
you'll have done me a favor.

Ako zapovedni način prevedete
na jezik želje da biva neispunjena,
poveriću vam svog psa.
Kad pomislite da me nema,
ako se ne upitate o poreklu
mojih zahteva,

voleću vas više
nego žive.

If you translate the imperative mood
into the language of a wish
that doesn't wish to be fulfilled,
I'll entrust you with my dog.
When you think I'm not there,
if you don't question the origins
of my requests,

I'll love you more
than the living.

ČARLI

(moj pas)
ima svog psa
(to sam ja).

CHARLIE

(my dog)
has his own dog
(that's me).

POREKLO OBLIKA

Skupljaš se u strahu od banalnosti.
Sažimaš se u naporu da ne izneveriš
gostoprimstvo ljušture.

Tako nastaje biser
i neko kamenje
neosporno drago.

THE ORIGIN OF FORM

You curl up in fear of banality.
You compress yourself striving not to betray
the shell's hospitality.

Thus arises a pearl
and some stone
indubitably precious.

DRAGI BOG

moj lični nosač tajni.

Na njega mislim
kad tebi želim dobro
a sebi nemoguće.

DEAR GOD

my personal bearer of secrets.

I think of him
when I wish the best to you
but the impossible to myself.

ANESTEZIJA

Mala velika moja,
Igla je neupitno dokazala
Čak i tebi, nepokornoj:
Ni san ne može bez bola.

Laborantkinja je rekla pružite dlan
I jedva našla pritoku u delti vena;
Doktorka se sažela u tri pitanja:
O majci, tebi, strahu kao opijatu.

Posle samo 20 minuta, ukucala je
U novootvoreni fajl nazvan mojim imenom:
Nalaz krvi regularan,
Pacijentkinja se žali na insomniju,
Upućena na razgovor sa specijalistom.

Dok je tipkala naglas ponavljajući reči,
Ja, zatečena sporim protokom vremena,
Doživela sam čitav somnabulni omnibus:

Majka je bila jedan te isti profil
Što se naglo pojavljuje, što je i činila
Kada se najmanje nadam.
Ti, mlade oči ljubavi što zjape
Isprepadane intenzitetom
Prvi put činilo ti se neizdrživim.
Jedan medved me je jurio do kraja
Projekcije, sustigavši nekoliko puta poljubio,
Ipak, jednako se plašim, bežim, gubim dah.

ANAESTHESIA

My great little one,
The needle has proven it unquestionably
Even to you, so insubordinate:
Even sleep can't be without pain.

The lab tech said hold out your hand,
And hardly found a tributary in the delta of veins;
The doctor compressed things into three questions:
About my mother; you; fear as an opiate.

After only 20 minutes, she was typing
A newly opened file with my name in its title:
Blood test normal,
The patient complains of insomnia,
Referred to consultation with a specialist.

While she typed, repeating words aloud,
I, trapped by time's slow flow,
Lived a whole somnambulistic omnibus:

Mother had one and the same profile
Which suddenly repeats, which she did
When I least expect it.
You, young eyes of love that gape
Overwhelmed with intensity
The first time it seemed to you unbearable.
One bear was chasing me to the end
Of the projection, caught up and kissed me several times,
Nevertheless, I'm just as scared, I run, I'm out of breath.

Ukupni utisak nelagodnosti
Zbog uživanja u tome svemu.

Mala velika moja,
Dete doba u kojem je detinjstvo
Ništa osim predanja, istorijski zapis.
Ti, starija od mene, iako imaš sve zube
I još te ne zanimaju ni most ni krunica,

Ti, zaronjena u praistoriju ovog sunovrata,
Dok ja nepcima kusam med, više ne marim,
Mlada pameti prirodno smisla gladna,
Besmislom vremena toksinirana,
Kušnjo neodoljiva što mi se predaješ
Iskrenošću zavodljivo nespretnom,
Ljubim u mislima tamne kolutove
Groteskno srasle uz tvoj dečji lik.

Dok gledaš me kao davljenik,
Unapred pristala na ono što ja, ne starija,
Već voljena, treba da odlučim u vezi sa
Tehnikom izbavljenja,
Jedva dišem pod punom svešću
Da život mi poslednji put
Baca udicu, idealni mamac
Erotike totalne uzajamnosti.

Ja, u tvojim očima neustrašiva,
Suviše se bojim da bih te volela.

A summary imprint of awkwardness
Because of the pleasure in all that.

My great little one,
Child of an era in which childhood
Is nothing but a tradition, a historical record.
You, older than I am, though you have all your teeth
And you have no interest yet in either bridge or crown,

You, submerged in the prehistory of this turn of the sun
While I taste honey on my palate, I no longer care,
You, young mind naturally hungry for sense,
Intoxic with the nonsense of the time,
The irresistible trial that you pass along to me
With seductively awkward sincerity,
In my thoughts I kiss the dark circles
Grotesquely spreading on your childish visage.

While you look at me like a person drowning,
Agreed ahead of time to what I, no older,
Already loved, must decide in connection with
The rescue technique,
I hardly breathe with full awareness
That for the very last time life
Is throwing me a hook, the ideal lure
Of the erotica of total mutuality.

I, fearless in your eyes,
Am too afraid to love you.

Jer te volim. I to će trajati.
Jer nasuprot tvom uverenju,
Ne, nisam jača od poplava!

Ni približno snažna kao sumnja
Da bi tvoji prozirni prsti
Hladni od bujice strasti,
U odsudnom času koji sledi
Neumitno,

Sa mnom ili bez mene našli
Spasonosnu venu ponornica.

Because I love you. And that will endure.
Because, contrary to your conviction,
No, I am not stronger than the flood!

Nor anywhere as strong as the doubt
That your transparent fingers
Cold from torrents of passion,
In the hour of judgment that follows
Implacably,

Will with me or without me find
The underground rivers' saving vein.

ANATOMSKI ČAS

Ćutim.
Praznina nema usta. Sama neutoljenost.
Svojstvo utrobe.
Ogluvelo je doba od buke njenih creva.
Ćutim i tim rečima slavim
odsustvo ljubavi.
Jer svaki tren je svečanost,
a vreme tek spomenik prolaznosti.

Ćutimo.
Oni galame o zaverama i novom nameštaju.
Kupuju sobe. Pojačivače zvuka. Naoružavaju se.
Gađaju nas dahtanjem koje nikada nije bilo ljubavno.
Kupuju kupuju kupuju
najbrže letelice koje u sve kraćem roku
smanjuju planetu do glasine
o našem gubitništvu, o kraju sveta.
Ćutimo i tim rečima ispisujemo ovo poglavlje.
Jer samo beskrajna priča je priča,
a koja prizna svoj kraj to nije.

Ćutiš.
Posmatram kako ti raste kosa i vidim čin
promene
u revoluciji vlasi obojenih suncem.
Ne, nisi utihnula ljubavi.
Kupili su drvo samo zbog lista
sa tvojim zapisom da ga spalimo.
Jer samo što ne traži dokaz postoji,
spaseno od naše želje za trajanjem.

ANATOMY MOMENT

I keep quiet.
Emptiness is mouthless. Solely unconsoled.
A trait of the womb.
The noise from her intestines deafened the times.
I keep quiet and with those words I celebrate
love's absence.
For every moment is a ceremony,
while time's a mere memorial of transience.

We keep quiet.
They make noise about conspiracies and new furniture.
They buy rooms. Sound amplifiers. They arm themselves.
They aim at us with a gasp that never was amorous.
They buy they buy they buy
the fastest fliers that in ever less time
reduce the planet to a rumor
about how we are losers, about the end of the world.
We keep quiet, and with those words we write this chapter out.
For only an endless story is a story,
whereas one that admits its end is not.

You keep quiet.
I observe your hair growing and see the act
of change
in a revolution of bristles colored by sun.
No, you haven't passed away, love.
They bought a tree for the leaf alone
with your note that we should burn it.
For only that which seeks no proof exists,
rescued from our desire for duration.

BELA

U osnovi bela
Kada smo je našle, kučkarke –
Mi koje bazamo više od pasa
Optužene da »samo psima
Pomažemo, a šta je s ljudima?« –
Bila se tek okotila, blažena, iznurena
(Kako se to očituje na svim ženkama!)
I prljava od sigurnog blatišta
Tamo gde je male skrila kuja
Sa poverenjem u kal.

Nazvale smo je Bela zbog lepote
Veselosti što samo u očima postoji
I kada se druga mesta nade ugase.
Mi, koje teško zaplačemo,
Mada bismo često za dobar plač
Dale sve svoje kosti,
Ugledavši je kako jedva živa tetura
U istom času tiho rekosmo: »Aušvic«,
A iz jama zamandaljenih očima
Oslobodila se bar jedna suza.

Ostalo je priča opšta i nasušna
Prehrana reči kao i bilo koja:
Hrana, zdravlje, brlog, ljubav.
Ono što ni u moći govora
Ne nalazi utočište
Dom je trenutka spoja
Najdublje drame i kapi sreće.

BELLA

Basically white
When we bitchcatchers found her —
We who roam around more than the dogs
Reproached that "You only help dogs,
And what about people?" —
She had just whelped a litter, blissful, exhausted
(It's so obvious on all females!)
And filthy from the muddy sanctuary
Where the bitch had hidden her little ones
Trusting in the mud.

We named her Bella for the beauty
Of her cheerfulness that dwells only in the eyes
Even when other places of hope are extinguished.
We, who are slow to start crying —
Though often we'd give all our bones
For a good cry —
Noticing her as she staggered, barely alive,
We said softly all at once, "Auschwitz."
And we released at least one tear
From the pits of our shackled eyes.

The rest is a common story and the daily
Bread of a word like any other:
Food, health, a burrow, love.
What cannot find a refuge
Even in the power of speech
Is home to a moment of connection
Of deepest drama and a drop of happiness.

CARGO

Istovarili su nas na ovo kopno
I naredili – Slobodni ste!

Zastali smo kod reči istovar.
Iako bismo pre ili kasnije,
Što se kaže u svetu prtljaga,
Nastavili dalje.

Jer samo jeretik propoveda blizinu.
Kao što koren služi
Za vežbu iskorenjavanja.

Od tada je sve idealno na našoj parceli!
Svako ima ličnu nišu, jedinstveni broj.

I što je najvažnije, mogućnost
Otvaranja i zatvaranja po želji,
Počev od prozora, ekrana, u prošlosti
Intimnih brava sada javnih, do onoga
Što suparničko pleme naziva dušom.

CARGO

They unloaded us onto this land
And commanded: You're free!

We paused at the word *unload*.
Although sooner or later we would,
As they say in the world of baggage,
Have been rerouted farther.

For only a heretic preaches closeness.
Just as a root serves
For the practice of uprooting.

Since then everything's wonderful on our plot!
Everyone has a personal niche, an ID number.

And what's most important, the possibility
Of opening and closing as they wish,
Beginning with windows, screens, formerly
Intimate locks now public, right up to the one
That the rival tribe has named the soul.

CASA

Tu smo pravili veče jedne večeri književne
U zemlji kažu lepoj i ukletoj a možda jeste;
Podizali kuću po starinski pesma na pesmu
Na vino led stopio noćnu i jutarnju smenu.

Biva ta kuća sred plantaža organske tuge
Gde korov nasleđene smušenosti i druge
Radosti postojanja odsustvom se odomaće
Dok vernost saputničku uzgajaju samoće.

Tu smo pravili veče a čaše su vodile ljubav
Sa španskim pločicama, zelenom muzikom, sav
Svet zbio se željama začet sa strane unutrašnje, van
Motorna divljač razdavala krv za dnevne novine.

David je recitovao Eliota, Biserka prosula Vislavu;
Znojem poprskani slušali kako nam on kaže Livadu;
Ana je hitnula cipele, zaigrala tango za zlatnu ribicu;
Beše posvećenosti. Ivana dahom lotosa izronila školjku.

To veče je našlo svoje more i dobâ vodolija,
Žene su bacale afričke cvetove sa haljina,
Stigla je Indija, zavrteo se brazilski čačak,
Ušetao je pas, na otirač priseo mačak.

Popadaše mitovi s oduškom, raj i Vaviloni
U slobodnom plesu izmirenih reči i naravi;
Dunav je pustio glas ispod odbačenih boca, utopljenika.
Beše ispovesti. Dugo sputavana stigla serenada do Nila.

CASA

Here we held a night one literary evening
In a land they call beautiful and cursed, and perhaps it is;
We raised a house the old way, poem on poem
Ice in wine melted the night and morning shifts.

That house takes place on a plantation of organic sorrow
Where the heirloom weed of confusion and of the other
Joy of existence through absence is domesticated
While isolations nurture a fellow-traveling fidelity.

Here we conceived an evening whereas the cups made love
With Spanish tiles, with green music, the entire world
Emerged begotten with desires from inside, outside
Motorized wildlife passed around blood for the daily papers.

David recited Eliot, Biserka was strewing Wisława;
Sprinkled with sweat we listened as he told us Livada;
Ana kicked off her shoes to tango for a golden fish;
There were dedications. Ivana's lotus breath came up a shell.

That evening found its sea and the age of Aquarius,
The women flung African flowers from their dresses,
India arrived, a Brazilian round dance spun like a thistle,
A dog strolled in, a tomcat sat down on the mat.

Myths dropped by with a breather, paradise and Babylons,
In a free twist of agitated words and natures;
The Danube hooted under tossed plastic bottles, drowned.
There were confessions. A long chained serenade reached the Nile.

Doživljaj, brate, mani događaje! – Bane je iza aparata
Posmatrao tajne dodire nasumičnih i propisanih koraka.
Plesala sam s Inkom, osmesi Antalije namiriše prijatelje
Odaslate gestom vina od neznanog sa Rta Dobre Nade.

Ta kuća osta naša istorija, religija, mapa, neprekidna fregata
Iako samo jednom, a možda ni tada? za šankom beše debata
Da li se kelner zove Rikardo ili Roberto? Očima toreadora
Rafaelo je mamio bika ili već neko ime strasti nad strastima:

Bez naziva ulice, broja, nezavisno od grada
Nastanili smo bojama oblike najvećeg zidara:
Majstora koji ume da nadigra zabran pogleda:
Prisnost izlije čas uzajamnosti kockica leda.

The experience, brah, lures happenings! — At the camera Bane
Watched the secret contacts of random and regulated steps.
I danced with an Inca, Anatolia's smiles perfumed the friends
A stranger sent with a gesture of wine from the Cape of Good Hope.

That house remained our history, religion, map, an uninterrupted frigate
Though only once, and maybe not even then? at the counter a debate:
Was the waiter's name Ricardo or Roberto? With the eyes of a toreador
Rafaelo lured the bull or else some name of passion above passions:

Without a street sign, a number, regardless of the city,
We settled into the greatest builder's forms with colors:
Of the master craftsman who can outplay a banned look:
Intimacy pours out an instant of mutual ice cubes.

DANAK

Daleko od ulice
Jedan trotoar i santimentar i po
Ograde u vidu paukove mreže
Zalogajem okućnice čuvana
Profesorka sadi cveće.

Dan u proleću.
Svako bi sa ulice taj prizor
Iako razlomljen
Metalnim ukrštanjem linija
Doživeo idilično.
Mačke zaigrane u mladoj travi.
Saksije od godina prošlih
Ukazuju na ritual.

Očev pribor podseća na uzor baštovanstva.
Kako je on odgajao, lagano, »s ljubavlju«
Naglašavajući pomalo zadrt, ali nežno
Uranja prstima u vlažnu zemlju
Naizgled više puta mereći
Palcem dubinu doma korena.

Prolaznici zaštićeni od pomisli
Da ti nežni dodiri
Od sinoć ruše zid
Brige poistovećene sa korovom –
Brige osnažene divljenjem
Onome što niče tek oboreno.

DAY

As far from the street
As a sidewalk plus half an inch
Railings in the image of a spiderweb
A teacher preserved by this morsel
Of a yard is planting flowers.

A day in spring.
From the street anyone would experience
That sight although diffracted
By the metal intersection of lines
As an idyllic one.
Cats playing in the young grass.
Flowerpots from past years
Indicate a ritual.

Her father's tools recall a model of gardening.
How he would raise, easily, "with love"
Stressing somewhat stubborn, but gently
She plunges fingers into the damp soil
Her thumb apparently measuring several times
The depth of the root's home.

Passersby protected from the thought
That those gentle touches
Have since last night been knocking down a wall
Of worry equated with a weed —
A worry strengthened by marveling
At what's knocked down barely sprouted.

Ćerka ni jutros nije došla.
Ne vredi da je traži –
Deca spavaju u ovo doba.
Celu noć su predano lomila
Klupe, kante za smeće i grane
Mladog drveća.

Pila su deca kao zidari u podne
Tamo gde njihovo neimarstvo
Motri nevidljiva policija,
Gde se bes na ispraznost kalemi,
A ruka najamnika u zoru pokupi srču.

Gde sam pogrešila? – pita se kao i svaka majka
Iz vremena kada su deca i majkama pripadala,
Komšije uljudno opominjale zbog glasne muzike.
Zašto bi odjednom zaboravila rođendane
Spravljane više dana unapred?
Da li je moguće da za svoje dete
Ovoliko ne postojim?

Od danas, tačnije, od ove muškatle,
Predana ravnodušnosti
Na sve generacije izvedene na put,
Bukete o praznicima, zapaćenu
Pristojnost sada uglednih građana
Amerike, Australije, Novog Zelanda,
»Često mislim na vas« razglednice.

Pogleda pobodenog u saksiju,
Profesorka otire sitno grumenje
Sa okrnjenih rubova.
Šoljicom za kafu poji buduće mladice.

Her daughter wasn't home this morning either.
It's no use looking for her —
Children are sleeping at this time of day.
All night long they were devotedly smashing
Benches, trash cans and the branches
Of young trees.

The children were drinking like bricklayers at noon
There where their lack of walls
Is surveilled by invisible police,
Where a demon vaccinates them for emptiness,
While at dawn the hireling's hand picks up the heart.

Where did I go wrong? — she asks just like every mother
From the times when children belonged to mothers too,
Neighbors politely told them to turn down their loud music . . .
Why would she suddenly forget birthdays
Planned so many days in advance?
Is it possible that I don't exist
To such an extent for my own child?

Starting today or, rather, starting from this geranium,
Devoted to indifference
To all the generations guided onto the right path,
Bouquets at the holidays, the rooted
Decorum of the now respectable citizens
Of America, Australia, New Zealand,
Postcards with "I often think of you."

Her gaze pinned to a flowerpot,
The teacher wipes a tiny lump
From the chipped edges.
She waters the future shoots with a coffee cup.

Ćerka će jednom doći
Da se presvuče, istušira, pita
Ima li nešto za jelo u ovoj kući?!
Potom će ponovo ući u rasad
Krda maloletnika koje se složno valja
Niz ulice poput odronjenog kamenja.
Urlaju, psuju, gutaju s nogu tečna
I tvrda, sitna đubriva popularno
Nazvana »ekseri« velike moći
Pretnje prolaznicima.
Građani ustupaju mesto strahu,
Dok organi nekog novog reda
Obezbeđuju brzi rast kolone
U stasalu bujicu.
I tako teku divlji dani
Kažu svuda u svetu.

Ko mi je oduzeo dete? – pita se kao i svaka majka
Iz bivšeg porodičnog dvorišta
Sasvim nalik ovom
Sa svežim rasadom
Iza ograde u vidu paukove mreže.

Dok prstima potkopava zid brige
Naizgled sadeći cveće,
Vidi mlade vojnike u azijskim pustinjama,
Devojčice polunage, gotovo slepe
Pod šminkom precvale, slične –
Kao da ih je sve ona rodila.

At some point her daughter will show up
To change her clothes, take a shower, ask
Is there anything to eat in this house?!
Afterwards she'll go back to the seedbed
Of the underage herd that rolls in unison
Down the streets like falling rocks.
They holler, swear, swallow standing the liquid
And the solid, tiny packets of dirt popularly
Known as "uppers" of great power
For threatening passersby.
The citizens make way for fear,
While the force of some new order
Ensures the speedy growth of a column
In stagnant torrent.
And thus the wild days flow past
They say, everywhere in the world.

Who took away my child? — she asks herself like every mother
From a former family yard
Entirely like this one
With the fresh seedbed
Behind the railing in the image of a spiderweb.

While her fingers undermine the wall of worry
While apparently planting flowers,
She sees young soldiers in the deserts of Asia,
Little girls half naked, almost blind
Under layers of makeup fading, similar —
As if she had given birth to them all.

Obeležene
Prstenom na samoj sredini tela,
Posađene
Na jednoj ili obema
Golim nogama
Nečijih bogatih očeva.

Printed
With a ring at the body's very center,
Planted
On one or both
Naked legs
Of someone's wealthy fathers.

OČAJNA PESMA

Ovim putem apelujem,
Ne libim se da preklinjem
Koga vi odaberete u narodnom
Krugu ponavljanja volje
Za moć ministra poezije:

Hoću da budem debela! Neka se vidi
Koliko me ima. Manite me diktata
Mršavosti, fitnes stihova, trenera
Knjiga pesama za zdrav život nacije.
Sobom se hranim, pa kakva ispadnem!

Izabrani, mirne duše konkurišite za mis
Nove osećajnosti bezvremenog čoveka.
Unapred sam odustala od scene i pobede.
Kako ste mogli da me previdite, ovoliku,
Redukovani, eksperimentalni, bez teksta?

Ne tražim puno, samo pomilovanje
Za višak težine, za naslage polisemije,
Za nas koji ne umemo da pevamo izvan
Svog jezika polifonije, neprevodive
U stilu nemarnog, prirodnog odevanja,

Za bluz improvizacije na licu mesta.
Za pušačko kašljucanje pevačice.
I za udeo smisla u praznom hodu, kao u šali
Pola zbilje što dobro dođe u gladi od gustog
Vina u kojem istina sušta usamljena obitava.

DESPERATE POEM

This time I make an appeal,
I don't hesitate to plead
Whoever you elect in the people's
Next round of reiteration of will
To the powers of minister of poetry:

I want to be tubby! Let everyone see
How much of me. Spare me the dictates
Of slenderness, fitness verses, coaches
Of poetry books for healthy life of the nation.
I feed on myself, so however I come out!

Chosen ones, go ahead and compete with calm souls
To be Miss New Sensitivity of the timeless person.
I've given up the stage and conquest in advance.
How could you overlook me, so substantial,
You reduced, experimental, textless ones?

I don't ask much, just to be pardoned
For excess heaviness, the spare tire of polysemy,
For those of us who cannot sing outside
Our language of polyphony, untranslatable
In a style of careless, natural dressing,

For blues improvisation right on the spot.
For the sultry singer's smoker's cough.
And for meaning's share in an idle stroll, as if in jest
The half truth that's handy in hunger from the thick
Wine where genuine lonely *veritas* resides.

Dopustite da nismo u obavezi
Produžetka veka makrobiotikom.
Bar pokoji pokvaren zub nam oprostite.
Mirno da ločemo pivo iz limenke bez komentara
Za vitke noge vaših vinskih čaša s ledom do pola.

Let it be that we are not obligated
To extend our age macrobiotically.
Forgive us at least the occasional rotten tooth.
Let us calmly slurp beer from the can without comment
On the slenger legs of your wineglasses, half full of ice.

DNEVNIK SITNIH NEZGODA

Jaje
koje sam u snu ukrala iz gnjezda
predskazalo je sudar s konjem
na pešačkom prelazu.
Nisam shvatila.

Ugruvana i još sanjiva
sputana
neprijatnom obavezom da budem pametna
sačekala sam red za mleko
ali umesto belog mlaza
poispadaše grudve tuđe
ustajale površnosti.

Pomislih *takve gluposti*
mogu se dogoditi samo meni!
I vratih se da zamenim mleko.

Onda je počeo da zvoni telefon.
Jedna duša me je zapovednim glasom
pozvala na sopstvenu sahranu.
Dobar prijatelj u žurbi
naručio je pesmu.
Poslednja nežnost
obavestila me je preko sekretarice
da grešim u proceni.

I moj privatni usamljenik
zaćutao je nekoliko puta.

A DIARY OF MINOR TROUBLES

The egg
I stole from a nest in my dream
foretold my crash into a horse
at the pedestrian crossing.
I didn't catch on.

Aching and still dreamy
hobbled
by the unpleasant duty to be clever
I waited in line and bought milk
but instead of a white stream
what tumbled out were clots of alien
stale superficiality.

I thought *stupid things like this*
could happen only to me!
And went back to exchange the milk.

Then the phone started ringing.
A soul with a commanding voice
invited me to its own funeral.
A good friend in a hurry
placed an order for a poem.
The ultimate tenderness
informed me via its secretary
that I was erring in assessment.

And my private hermit
fell silent several times.

Neko iz komšiluka je pucao.
Neko drugi se zaljubio
i pokušao da se ubije.
Policija nas je sve ispitala.
Koristeći pometnju
deca su pušila u podrumu.

U među vremenu stiglo je pismo
iz Amerike. Jesen je ovde divna
pisao je stric i lišće crvenožuto.
Ali kada počneš da ga sakupljaš
sva čarolija nestaje
i zamisli
posle šezdeset godina iskustva
mama je rešila da ne vozi!

Istoga dana javili su
da je rođak operisan posle saobraćajne nesreće.
Tom prilikom dodali su da mu je neko ukrao baj pas.
Javili su greškom
da je muž moje sestre ranjen na frontu.
Teško. Svi smo plakali.
Po podne su se izvinili.
I ona se javila
On je samo faza u mom životu!
Aha, rekla sam.

Oštreći reči u jednom razgovoru
posekla sam jezik.
Dobila sam telegram od pozitivnog junaka
Do-sta-mi-je-sve-ga!
Na mnogim vratima u gradu osvanulo je
NE VRAĆAM SE!

Someone in the neighborhood was shooting.
Someone else fell in love
and tried to kill himself.
The police interrogated all of us.
Kids were smoking in the cellar
taking advantage of the ruckus.

Meanwhile a letter arrived
from America. Autumn is gorgeous here
wrote my uncle and the leaves red and yellow.
But when you start raking them
all the enchantment disappears
and just imagine
after sixty years of experience
mama has decided to stop driving!

The same day they sent word
that our relative had surgery after a car crash.
They added by the way that someone had stolen his bye pass.
They sent word by mistake
that my cousin's husband had been wounded on the front.
Bad news. We all cried.
In the afternoon they apologized.
And she sent word too
This is just a phase in my life!
Uh-huh, I said.

As I sharpened the words in one conversation
I cut my tongue.
I got a telegram from a good guy:
I've-had-it-up-to-here!
The sign rose on many doors in the city
NOT COMING BACK!

Pred veče
dečak u brzim kolima pregazio je psa.
U autobusu su mi ukrali novčanik
sa poslednjim apoenom razumevanja.
Sve vas treba pobiti! vikala sam
                              ostatak dana.

U horoskopu su me upozorili
da suviše mislim o novcu –
ljubav – ništa – zdravlje – premor.
Mama je spremila masnu večeru
To je zbog ove situacije!
Nervozna sam.
Zaboravljam.

Pokušala sam da čitam
ali tajne ljubavi
pronađoše odličnu zabavu
u mojim nervima.
Kada se polica u ponoć srušila
kazaljke su se poklopile.
Nisam shvatila.

Koristeći jeftine impulse
zvao je bivši prijatelj
iz Rusije. *Ovde je super!*
naglašavao je svaki slog.
I ja sam dobro rekoh.

Još sam pribeležila za novu priču
rečenicu *Ona se opija svojom patnjom*
ali mi to ne shvatamo.

In late afternoon
a boy in a fast car ran over a dog.
My wallet was stolen in the bus
with the final denomination of understanding.
You should all be killed! I shouted

                                        the rest of the day.

My horoscope warned me
that I was thinking too much about money —
love — nothing — health — exhaustion.
Mama cooked a fatty dinner
It's because of this situation!
I'm nervous.
I keep forgetting things.

I tried to read
but my secret loves
found an excellent amusement
in my nerves.
When the shelf came crashing down at midnight
the clock hands touched.
I didn't catch on.

Making use of cheap minutes
a former friend called
from Russia. *It's just great here!*
He stressed every syllable.
I'm doing fine as well, I said.

I also noted down for a new story
the sentence *She gets drunk on her suffering*
but we don't catch on.

Umesto kestenja i stihova
u šetnji ubrah napev
koga ne mogu da se rešim
Možda je moglo! Možda je moglo!

Zaspala sam uprkos istovremenom
histeričnom napadu auto-alarma.

Grad u kojem se sve to dešavalo
pokazivao je znake života
na sve samim pogrešnim mestima.

Instead of chestnuts and poems
as I strolled I picked up a melody
that I can't get rid of
Maybe it could have! Maybe it could have!

I fell asleep despite the simultaneous
hysterical attack of a car alarm.

The city where all this happened
was showing signs of life
in all the wrongest places.

DRAMA

Ivani Milankovoj

Malo ko zna
Ta mesta u grčkim brdima
Gde istina nema mora ali oduvek teku rečice
I fontane predskazuju prošlost tako uverljivo
Da se sve vreme dešava,
A vrbe i lokvanji kao da samo zato postoje
Uspevaju na fotografijama.

Meštani ne obraćaju pažnju
Na lepotu sa kojom žive.
Turisti nisu obavešteni.

Poneki krstić na geografskoj karti
Označava zid crkve koji ume da se ljubi;
Taverne se razlikuju po boji stolica
Spremne da ugoste sva raspoloženja
Zatvaraju se tek kad poslednje sedište
Licem prione na sto upravo na mestu
Gde se do maločas dlan mirio sa čim treba.

Ljudi prođu mnogo toga
Sve i kad im kretnje staju
Kod prvog vinograda.
Ili su prevalili put ne opazivši putovanje.
Tek u daljim godinama osete da ima nešto
U tim mestima gde se može voleti
Ukus vode i sira.

DRAMA

to Ivana Milankova

Few people know
Those places in the hills of Greece
Where truth has no sea but streams have flowed forever
And fountains foretell the past so persuasively
That it happens all the time,
While it seems as if the willows and waterlilies exist only
To look great in photographs.

The locals pay no attention
To the beauty they live with.
The tourists are not informed.

The occasional cross on the geographical map
Signifies a church wall that knows how to be kissed;
The taverns are distinguished by the color of chairs
Ready to host all kinds of moods
They close only when the final seat
Is set face-down on the table right in the place
Where until just now a hand was resting with what was needed.

People pass through a lot
As well when their movement stops
At the first vineyard.
Or they made the journey without noticing the traffic.
Only in years ahead they feel that there is something
In those places where one can love
The taste of water and cheese.

I zaljube se u prijatnu
Dovoljnost takvih dana
Kada pitanja ne nalaze uporište
U mestima gde niko ne govori o ljubavi
I gde svako može kao i što ne mora da zna
Pismo bora na koži dugovekih
Meštana i stabla masline.

Tamo gde smo naizgled zalutali
Netaknute počivaju priče.

And they fall in love in the pleasant
Plenitude of such days
When questions find no foothold
In places where no one talks about love
And where everyone can and doesn't have to know
The writing of wrinkles on the skin of long-lived
Locals and the trunks of olive trees.

There where we seemed to have lost our way
The stories repose untouched.

FADO TRISTE

Kad nedostaješ nisi to ti.
Nema onoga što je bilo.
Fado.

Moja tajna ljubav
prolazi kao tramvaj
želja da zavolim bol.
Frida.

Putovanje pejzaža kroz prozor voza.
Plavo ko zna zašto i ne uvek.
Neobavezno.

Primeti obilje naočara za sunce. Onako.
Preterana osetljivost oslepljuje.
Snađi se i budi.

San posle sna.
Tam tam.
To kako ulica razume samoću

ne da se ni zamisliti
ali prijaš mi
mi buen amor.

FADO TRISTE

When I miss you it isn't you.
What was no longer is.
Fado.

My secret love
passes like a streetcar
my desire to come to love pain.
Frida.

The journey of a landscape through a train window.
Blue who knows why and not always.
Optionally.

Notice the abundance of sunglasses. No special reason.
Excessive sensitivity is blinding.
Find yourself a way and be.

Dream after dream.
Tam tam.
The way the street understands loneliness

can't even be imagined
but you please me
mi buen amor.

PECANJE

Sedi starac na keju i peca.
Za mene je on starac,
Za mnoge sam ja već starica, tako da:
Sedi na keju dečak koji je prikupio mnogo godina i peca.

On se smeši sve vreme. U tome je Pesma.
Ulov je sporedan, ljudi tako-tako.
Ali taj spoj neba, vode i spokoja!
Taj trofej zrelosti, dostojno osvojen.

Prilazi mu čovek, pita: – Prijatelju, grize li šta?
– Kako-kad, prijatelju, kako-kad.
Čovek uljudno osmehom uzvrati na osmeh.
Klimne glavom, u znak poštovanja, odlazi.

Posmatram, pomalo voajerski, ćutim.
Uživamo u vrhunskom koncertu:
Mrmor reke, povremeni zaron gnjurca,
Retke deonice brodskih sirena, dozivanja
Dece, pasa – glasove prima i rastače vetar.

I usred te savršene kompozicije, dakle,
Melodije koju ništa ne može da poremeti,
Dečak pogleda mlađu devojčicu, izusti:
– Sine, šta te to toliko muči?

Zaboravljam na stid, breme što ga poput šlepera
Vučem u dugoj plovidbi iz najranijih dana, odmah odgovaram:
– Izdaja, gospodine, izdaja najbližeg! Ili sam bar ja verovala da je . . .

FISHING

An old man's sitting on the quay and fishing.
For me he's an old man,
For many I'm already an old woman, and so:
A boy who has amassed a lot of years is sitting on the quay, fishing.

He's smiling the whole time. That contains the Poem.
The catch is secondary, the people more or less.
But that compound of sky, water and tranquility!
That trophy of maturity, mastered with dignity.

Someone comes up to him, asks: "Hey friend, are they biting?"
"From time to time, my friend, from time to time."
The person courteously exchanges a smile for a smile.
Nods, as a sign of respect, and walks away.

I watch a while, a little voyeuristically, I keep quiet.
We take pleasure in an excellent concerto:
The river's murmur, the grebe's occasional dive,
Scarce measures from ship sirens, voices calling
Children, dogs — the wind takes up and scatters the voices.

And amid that perfect composition, therefore,
Of a melody nothing can disrupt,
The boy on the quay looks at the younger girl, utters:
"What's bothering you so much, dear?"

I forget embarrassment, the burden I've hauled like a tugboat
On a long voyage since the earliest days, I answer at once:
"Betrayal, sir, betrayal of the closest person! Or at least I thought . . ."

Starina umalo da prasne u smeh. Bori se s njim.
Ja samo što nisam pala sa ivice očaja, borim se s tim.
On se rva kao sa sabljarkom iz romana,
Klati se na keju, na samom rubu krivice.

Ali mir na reci se brzo uspostavlja.
Reka zanavek briše sve prethodeće.
I mi sedimo jedno kraj drugog opuštenih
Nerava, mišića, stenta, metala u nozi,
Šta je već ko sa sobom ovde doneo.

Ćutimo i nastavljamo da slušamo
Koncert nad koncertima.
U jednom taktu, on me pogleda,
Sa osmehom, razume se, te reče:

– Zar nisi čula šta sam rekao onom?

– Kom? Prijatelju u prolazu?

– Svejedno.

– Ne pamtim, šta ste rekli?

– Grize, sine, grize kako-kad.

The old man all but breaks into laughter. He fights with it.
I've all but fallen from the brink of despair, I fight with that.
He wrestles as if with the huge swordfish from the novella,
Teeters on the quay, on the very edge of guilt.

But peace on the river is quickly restored.
The river forever erases everything from before.
And we sit one beside the other with relaxed
Nerves, muscles, stents, metal in the leg,
Everything each one here has brought along.

We keep quiet and continue listening
To the concerto of concertos.
In one beat, he takes a look at me,
With a smile of course, then he says:

"Didn't you hear what I said to that one?"

"Who? Your friend passing by?"

"Whoever it was."

"I don't remember, what did you say?"

"They bite, dear, they bite from time to time."

* * *

40 dana nisam napisala pesmu,
Ja, koja ne brojim, dane naročito,
Upamtila sam početak neizrecivog.
40 dana slušam savršenstvo
Smene nemih stihova
Koji se ne daju omesti rečima.
Očarana stvaranjem
Neprestanog
Prerušavanja ničega u sve.

* * *

40 days I haven't written a poem,
I, who do not count — especially days —
Fixed in memory the start of the unutterable.
40 days I've been listening to the perfection
Of mutely alternating verses
That won't let themselves be tripped up by words.
Enchanted by the creation
Of an incessant
Disguise of nothing as everything.

IME REKE
(odlomak iz poeme)

Vislavi

I

Uvek različita
reka
po svojoj prirodi
ne nalikuje drugoj.

Sama je svoje ime, mada
razume mnogo toga, pa i naše razloge za geografiju:
muku kartografije,
sve te savršene linije,
strast ograđivanja,
zidove sa napuklinom već sutradan,
žice, burad, zastavice, kamenje
preseljeno iz nekog drugog pejzaža,
i zimzelen u stroju
i usnulog stražara –
čitav taj ritual prisvajanja.

Njen tok je pun obzira i stoga krivudav.
Naučila je da traje između.
Otkako je nastala ne liči na sebe jer stalno odlazi.
Tako i uspeva da ostane u mestu. Bar prividno.
Bar koliko mi vidimo.

THE RIVER'S NAME
(excerpt from a long poem)

to Wisława

I

Always dissimilar
the river
by her nature
resembles no other.

She is herself her own name, although
she understands a lot, our reasons for geography too:
the anguish of cartography,
all those perfect lines,
the passion of enacting borders,
walls already cracked the next day,
wires, barrels, pennants, stones
resettled from some other landscape,
and evergreen in array
and the watchman who's fallen asleep —
that whole ritual of appropriation.

Her course is full of consideration and therefore meandering.
She has learned how to last in between.
Ever since she arose she isn't like herself for she is constantly departing.
So she manages to stay in place. At least apparently.
At least as far as we can tell.

Reka mora biti tu.
Svi plove rekom osim nje same.
Oduvek je tako: jedni se kreću, drugi pokreću.
Reka ne razmišlja o sudbini i pravdi.
Suviše je toga videla da bi poredila.

Dinamična i statična
izmiče dijagnozama.
Nikada bolesna jer nikada zdrava.
Postojeća.

Ljudi, koji bi stalno da se vrate,
često su o njoj pisali.
Zastupljena je gotovo u svakom mitu.
Poverili su joj toliko pepela
da jedva stiže da razloži svu tu čast.
Dive joj se
tako što zamišljaju da plavi.

Evo, i u ovom času
slikar studira njenu boju,
vernik pere noge,
jelen pije,
utopljenik se uspešno krije,
seljanka sa zadignutom suknjom
žali se na novu trudnoću,
vrba čitav dan obožava sebe,
a turista se raspituje
da li je bezbedna? Kako kad.

Sve njeno je u njoj.
Sama je svoja granica.
Osim toka, nema drugih dimenzija.

The river must be here.
Everyone sails in the river except for her.
It's always been like that: some move around, others move things.
The river doesn't ponder fate and justice.
She has seen too many things to compare them.

Dynamic and static
she dodges diagnoses.
Never ill, since never well.
In existence.

People, who always want to go back,
have often written about her.
She's represented in almost every myth.
They have entrusted so much ash to her
that she hardly manages to scatter all that honor.
They marvel at her
so that they imagine she is flooding.

Here, at this moment too
a painter is studying her color,
a believer is washing his feet,
a deer is drinking,
a drowned person successfully hides,
a peasant woman with her skirt hiked up
complains about her new pregnancy,
a willow admires itself the whole day,
while a tourist inquires
is she safe? Depends on when.

Everything that's hers is in her.
She is her own border.
Besides flowing, she has no other dimensions.

Iskupljuje prostiranjem.
Iz vazduha se mogu videti
sve njene pritoke:
sva njena raspeća.

Ne odgovara opisu jer nema pozu.
Ume da postoji bez tumačenja.
U ležištu koje je po svojoj meri stvorila
ima gde da odloži višak značenja.

Ona nije metafora.
Reka je reka.
Reči joj ne mogu ništa.

Gleda svoja posla – pravo u nebo.
Ne gubi vreme
otkako postoji
obavlja najteži od svih poslova:
pokreće sebe.

I teži moru.

Reka zna da je njena čežnja u njoj.
Ona žudi za morem.
More o tome nema pojma.

Privlačna za siromašne i tužne
zato što je jednostavna.
Njena raskoš je u iskustvu
koje se ne vidi.

She redeems it by spreading.
From the air you can see
all her tributaries:
all her crucifixions.

She doesn't match description for she has no pose.
She knows how to exist without commentary.
In the place to lie down she has created for her own dimensions
she has room to put off an excess of significance.

She's not a metaphor.
The river is a river.
Words will never hurt her.

She looks to her own business — straight into the sky.
Hasn't wasted time
since she arose
she's been doing the hardest of all jobs:
she moves herself.

And tends toward the sea.

The river knows that her longing is in herself.
She yearns for the sea.
The sea has no idea about it.

Attractive to the poor and sad
because she's simple.
Her pageantry is in the experience
that isn't visible.

Bliska kao dodir i istovremeno
ko zna gde.
Već je stigla svuda.

Ponornica kad zatreba
i primer ulivanja.
Izvor na pravom mestu.

Uvek dublja od dileme:
da li je posmatramo ili ona posmatra nas.

(...)

Close as a touch and simultaneously
who knows where.
She has already arrived everywhere.

A diver when it's necessary
and an example of inflowing.
A wellspring rightly placed.

Always deeper than the dilemma:
are we observing her or is she observing us.

(. . .)

INKA

Nisam stigla da budem drevna.
Protrčala sam kroz samo nekoliko
Vekova, dok sam jurcala kroz šume,
Pentrala se sa dečacima na visove
Odakle se najbolje vidi
Kad se odrasli ljube.

Moj narod je bio odeven u boju zlata
I prašine. Zato smo se klanjali suncu.
Od pera papagaja pravili ukosnice.
Žuti i crveni i zeleni plodovi
Prirasli su nam uz šake kao kapi
Vodopada na usnama – nije postojao
Ritual ručka.

Živeli smo bez reči za
Obuću, časovnik, ljubav.
Dečaci su me podučili visokim tonovima
Pojedinačnih dodira pampa i stopala.
Živeli smo po zvuku.
Nismo opisivali. Kliktali smo.
A kada ni bi nam kondor ukazao čast
Novim izvođenjem svog leta,
Nepomični, zadržali smo dah.
Ništa osim lepote nije moglo
Da nas zaustavi, dok postojali.

Kasnije, kada su nas poništili i nazvali
Civilizacijom, divili se starom

THE INCA

I had no time to be ancient.
I went skipping through only several
Centuries, while I dashed around forests,
Clambered with boys up to the heights
From which you can see the best
When grown-ups are exchanging kisses.

My people were clad in the color of gold
And dust. Therefore we worshipped the sun.
We made hairpins from parrot feathers.
Yellow and red and green fruits
Grew into our hands like the drops
Of waterfalls on our lips — we had no
Ritual of lunchtime.

We lived without words for
Footgear, timepiece, love.
The boys taught me the high tones
Of particular touches of pampa and feet.
We lived by sound.
We did not do descriptions. We cheered.
And whenever the condor did us the honor
Of newly performing a flight,
We held our breath, motionless.
Nothing but beauty was capable
Of stopping us, while we existed.

Later, when they destroyed us and called us
A civilization, marveled at the old

Računanju vremena,
Njihovi setni pesnici pevali
O bivšoj sreći svetlucavog naroda,
Izučavali su i ono što nazivaju
Idealnim oblikom vladanja.

Nisam stigla da budem tužna.
Život je posekao užas
Kratkim potezom.
Sablja je luđa od ruke kojom upravlja.
Ipak, kad pomislim na obučene zmije
I carske činije sa otmenim otrovima
Od privlegije postepenog kraja
Bolja je brzina narodske smrti,
Topla klanica od samice sarkofaga.

Dečaci i ja smo se osmehivali suncu.
Boginja konačnosti izvodila je ples
Lakih skokova sa okena na litice:
Vredi doživeti njen salto
Iz oblaka hop na leđa lame
I nazad uvek drugačije.

Ljudi boje mleka su jaukali
Usled napora, valjda,
Zamaha oštrih i teških
Neoplemenjenih metala,
Paljenja lomače,
Tovara odeće od zlata.

Way of accounting time,
Their sorrowful poets sang
Of the former joy of a radiant people,
They also studied what they called
An ideal form of governance.

I had no time to be sad.
Horror sliced through life
With a blunt gesture.
The sword is madder than the hand that wields it.
All the same, when I think of the trained snakes
And the regal bowls with noble poisons —
Better a people die speedily
Than be granted a gradual end,
Better warm slaughter than a sarcophagus, solitary.

The boys and I smiled at the sun.
The goddess of finality performed a dance
Of airy leaps from the ocean onto the cliffs:
It's worth experiencing her fatal *salto*
From the clouds, hop! onto the llama's back
And back again always differently.

The milk-colored people howled
From the effort, most likely,
Of swinging the sharp and heavy
Metals that had not been ennobled,
Of lighting the pyre,
Of the cargo of clothing of gold.

No, prošla je i ta predstava
Da bi se budući sećali
Uspešne scenografije.

Nebo je sada čisto i još lepše.
Kondor i dalje izvodi svoj let
Iz doba tihe, svetlucave dece.
Onda naglo nestane uplašen
Nepoznatim zvukom jecaja.
To, kažu, neka kraljica cvili
Misleći da je njen bog kažnjava
Jer vreme prolazi, a muž umoran
Od stalnih pohoda ne može više
Da čeka naslednika.

But that performance passed as well
So that later generations would recall
A successful screenplay.

Now the sky is clear and even lovelier.
The condor goes on carrying out its flight
From the era of quiet, gleaming children.
Then it suddenly disappears frightened
At the unfamiliar sound of moaning.
That, they say, is some queen weeping,
Thinking that her god is punishing her
For time is passing, while her husband weary
From constant conquests can no longer
Be waiting for an heir.

* * *

Bila si moj Japan, Grčka čak,
Normalno, Indija i Kina.
Bar da je srećan onaj ko te ima.
Da postoji, osim poriva – smak.

Da nisi prozrela sve privide
Čije si fatalno konačište.
Da ti se dala greška u koracima
Ljubavi suicidno neispavana.

Ti, ružo, samo jednom gola
Da bi me oživela, sahranila
Vejavicom latica, podsmehom
Na trn i lažno pravo bola.

Ostala si moj san, varka svitanja,
Nagonski poj ptica novoga dana.
Nemogućnost razočaravanja.
Ona koja vernost zaposeda.

* * *

You were my Japan, even my Greece.
Naturally, India and China.
If at least the one who has you is happy.
If, besides lust — the world's end exists.

If you haven't seen through all the simulacra
Whose fatal ending point you are.
If they called a foul on you in the steps
Of love, suicidally underslept.

You, my rose, naked only once
To make me come to life, to bury me
In a shower of petals, with a laugh
At the thorn and the false right of pain.

You have remained my dream, a trick of dawn,
The birds' instinct to sing on a new day.
Impossibility of disappointment.
She who has come to rule fidelity.

BEZEMLJAŠI

Mi smo nakot virusa dece.
I sve što dotaknemo, zakmeči.

Othranili smo roditelje,
Nemoćne klince od nas starije.
Začeli zemlju tako da ostane
Nedovršena.
Javno raskrinkali smisao prinova.

Sa nama je počelo da prestaje
Rađanje ustupivši mesto čežnji
Te svakoj totalnoj slobodi lučenja.
Sačuvali smo običaj nadevanja imena
Nikome nije jasno zbog čega.
Jedno je ljubav.

Živimo u večitoj školi. Učimo
Mitove. Jedan je Pripadanje.
Svaki naš korak je emigracija
Iz stranog u tuđe.
Stalno smo tu
Tako što nismo nigde.

Rešavamo ukrštene reči.
Podelili smo se
Na horizontalne i vertikalne.
Od tada smo usamljeni.
Stoga povremeno ratujemo
Kao i svi infantilno stareći.

THE LANDLESS

We're a litter of childhood diseases.
And everything we touch starts whimpering.

We brought up our parents,
Feeble kids older than we were.
Begat a land so it would remain
Uncompleted.
Openly unmasked the sense of acquisitions.

We witnessed a failing and falling
Birth rate, it gave way to yearning
And a total freedom of diffusion.
We preserved the custom of giving names
It's not clear to anyone why.
One of them is love.

We live in an eternal school. We study
Myths. One of them is Belonging.
Every step of ours is emigration
From the strange to the alien.
We're constantly here
So that we can be nowhere.

We solve crossed words.
We have split up
Into horizontal and vertical.
Since then we've been lonely.
Hence at times we make war
Aging like everyone, in an infantile manner.

Ranjivi smo. Saleću nas
Protuve sa obećanjem
Odrastanja u pravom spoju.
I kada smo umorni, nasednemo.
Dok manje umorni prozrevamo.
Sa stanovišta neizlečivog
Detinjstva
Svejedno je.

Izmislili smo svoj jezik.
Jedni se igraju nesporazuma,
Drugi su ovisni o dopisivanju,
Treći propovedaju telepatiju.
Naše knjige su lične poruke.
Poruka je sama po sebi višak.

Dato nam je svo vreme za razmišljanje.
Te tako svako od nas tačno zna šta želi
I to u nekoliko verzija,
Ubeđeni da je najvažnije imati San.

Kada pomenemo pusto ostrvo,
Ne znači da smo u afektu, ne!
Naš život je savršena meditacija.
Nego nas redovno napadne taj kliše
U vreme dugih mrazeva,
Suočavanja s natalnom golotinjom.

Mi, strahotno laka
Meta studenih pomama
Usled strgnutog priviđenja
Rodne grude.

We're touchy. They excite us
Vagabonds with the promise
Of growing up in the right connection.
And when we're tired, we buy it.
While less tired we see through it.
From the perspective of incurable
Childhood
It's all the same.

We've thought up a language of our own.
One group plays at misunderstandings,
A second is addicted to correspondence,
A third one advocates telepathy.
Our books are personal messages.
The message is surplus in itself.

We're given all of time for contemplation.
Therefore each of us knows what they want
And in several versions at that,
Convinced the main thing is to have a Dream.

When we mention the empty island,
It doesn't mean we're panicking, no!
Our life's a perfect meditation.
But that cliché attacks us regularly
During long cold snaps,
Confrontations with our natal nakedness.

We, a terribly easy
Target of frigid crazes
Due to the wrested illusion
Of native soil.

POSLEDNJA STANICA PREVODA

Vlasnica restorana u *Ulici lavova,*
U koji svraćam jer je blizu *Ulice lista* gde stanujem,
Mada preblizu pričama o logorima,
O mrtvim roditeljima i konvojima izbeglica
Od kojih neki još žive, evo, ovde u Beču,

Pita me da li sam primetila da je danas izrazito
Težak dan.
Pa kako je moguće da niste?!
Pa nama su se dve gošće onesvestile, odneše ih!
Dok je jedna pala mrtva ispred vrata
Restorana, kako saznajem kasnije.

Nisam. Meni je ovde tako neobično
Tiho.
Ja dolazim iz zemlje Uranije, kako reče Milankova,
Objašnjavam, u kojoj ljudi sasvim normalno lelujaju,
Svakodnevno i godinama
U hodu se pridržavaju za zgrade, nanizane automobile,
Jer ih vozila u pokretu gaze ili bar obaraju,
Jedni druge prevodimo preko ulice i –
Idemo dalje.

Ali zar niste čuli onolike sirene,
Onolika kola hitne pomoći zavijaju gradom ceo dan?

Čujem tišinu sve vreme
I jedva se na nju navikavam
Kao i na sve što oduvek volim.

THE LAST STATION OF TRANSLATION

The owner of a restaurant in *Lion Street*
Where I stop in since it's close to *Leaf Street* where I'm staying,
Although too close to stories of the camps,
Of dead parents and convoys of refugees
Some of whom still live right here in Vienna,

She asks me have I noticed that today is a distinctly
Difficult day.
Why how could it be that you haven't?!
Why two of our guests fainted, they were carried out!
While one had fallen down dead before the doors
Of the restaurant, as I later learn.

I haven't. Here for me it's unusually
Quiet.
I come from the land of Urania, as Milankova said,
I explain, where people quite regularly totter
Every day and for years on end
As they walk they hold on to buildings, lined-up cars,
For vehicles in motion crush them or just knock them over,
We help each other cross the street and —
On we go from there.

But haven't you heard so many sirens,
So many ambulances wailing the whole day through the city?

I hear quiet all the time
And I can hardly get used to it
Just like everything I've always loved.

Jedina nepoznanica su mi ptice pevačice:
Toliko ih je, tako divno pevaju,
Naročito s večeri,
A ja ne umem da prepoznam
Nijednu vrstu.

The only unfamiliar thing is the singing birds:
There are so many of them, they sing so wonderfully,
Especially come evening,
But I don't know how to recognize
A single kind.

JUTARNJA KAFA

Ljubavi, kako si se danas probudila?
Kao žena? Školjka? Dečak? Pas?
Lepa si.
Volela bih da se tako osećaš. Da li?
Želiš da mi prepričaš san?
Da li ti smeta što si Crnac
ili si očajna što tvoja bela koža ima 102 godine?
Brazil? Danas?
Prija li ti, kamenčiću, prvi jutarnji talas?
Nemoj da obraćaš pažnju na crvene repove,
obožavani koralu.
Svaki deo koristi pravo da bude telo.

Ipak kaži.
Želim i uvek o tebi sve da znam.
Jesi li prehlađena? (citat iz Almodovara)
Da li te više nego juče boli politička situacija? Kako kičma?
Hoćemo li danas da oplakujemo? Šta?
Kitove ili decu Avganistana?
Ono što odlažeš o majci? Opet bosa?
Banana, jabuka, ananas? Ne?
Zbog tebe verujem u sve. Reci.
I kada ćutiš reč je.
Samo ti možeš bilo šta.

Kao i da popiješ ovu kafu ćutke.
Kuvala sam je na vreme – čitave noći.
Uzavrela je u pravi čas – zorom.

MORNING COFFEE

My love, how did you wake up this morning?
As a woman? Seashell? A boy? A dog?
You're beautiful.
I'd love for you to feel that way. Do you?
Want to tell me what you dreamed?
Does it bother you that you're a Black man
or are you agonizing that your white skin is 102 years old?
Brazil? Today?
Does the first morning wave feel good to you, little pebble?
Don't pay attention to the red tails,
my adorable coral.
Every part makes use of the right to be a body.

Even so, say.
I want to know everything about you, and always.
Did you catch a chill? (a quote from Almodóvar)
Does the political situation hurt you more than yesterday? How's your spine?
Do we want to lament today? For what?
The whales or the children of Afghanistan?
What you're postponing about your mother? Barefoot again?
Banana, apple, pineapple? No?
Because of you I believe in everything. Say.
Even when you keep quiet it's a word.
Only you can be and do anything at all.

Just as you drink this coffee too without speaking.
I brewed it in time — whole nights.
It foamed up at the right moment — at dawn.

Kafa od mora ili od ljubavi. Kako god.
Tek su naslovi nevažni
sada kada si se probudila
u obliku ljubavi,
vratila vreme.

Ima ljubav oblik,
kao i svaka zamisao oseke i plime.
Ljubav ima sat
u opuštenom disanju peska.
Toliko zna, toliko davno
da je svako malo pospana.

Coffee from the sea or from love. However.
Only the titles are unimportant
now when you have woken up
in the shape of love,
have returned time.

Love has a shape,
like any brainchild of low tide and high tide.
Love has an hour
in the sand's relaxed breathing.
It knows so much, has known for so long
that every so often it's sleepy.

MOJ KRAJ

Ovde ne raste drveće života
Niti cveta limun žut.
Mirišu lipe uličarke,
Bog-hrast nadzire drum.

Naše su brazde opstajačke:
Zrno, krtola, luk.
Ljubav daleka poput mora,
Nedostojna za pošten pûk.

Naši od malena uče da kriju
Ako kuma poštedi kum,
I otac što pripuca na sina mora
Dalje – teši ga ratni drug.

Takva je klima. I položaj
Kao glavni pojam kraja.
Strane kulture žive svoj vek,
Ovde se niklo uzorava.

Čvrsta ruka nas drži kažu
Proizvođači dece i unuka
I put pod noge meću učenjaku
Da očuva se leb i motika.

Korov se slavi kao Učitelj
I svrhu nađe buđ.
Kost samo ljutom štencu daje
Da sutra osvane vuk.

MY NEIGHBORHOOD

Here, the Trees of Life don't grow,
Nor does the yellow lemon bud.
Street-walking lindens spread cologne,
The oak-god oversees the road.

Our furrows are just for subsistence:
A seed, an onion, a spud.
Like the sea, love's distant,
Not seemly for our honest folk.

Early on we're taught to cover
If a godfather spares a godfather,
And a dad who's shot at his son has gotta
Keep on — his war buddy calms him.

Such is the climate. With stature
As the main idea in my land.
There's a long life for foreign cultures,
Here every sprout's ploughed down.

We need a firm hand to guide us, say
Producers of kids and grandkids
And they set this path at the learner's feet—
You don't hoe, you get no bread.

A weed is famed as a Master
And even mildew finds its resolve.
Give the pup a bone only when it's angry
So tomorrow it will dawn a wolf.

TEHNIKA DISANJA

Iscelitelji se množe od postanja
Pošastima i boljkama u porastu
Stvarnim ili još nedomišljenim
Za koje najpre od njih saznamo.

Nastupilo je povoljno vreme
Zemlje rasprodate obećanjima
Prezenterima metoda nečuvenih
Što bržeg ozdravljenja.

Uglavnom obrazlažu bilje
Pojma nemajući kako diše

Niti ih zanima to što narod priča
Da lek i otrov samo skupa žive.

Učinak olako dokazuju
Pretpostavkom o saživljavanju
Travki i ljudske bahatosti
Koja pustoši nasumice.

Psihu propovedaju u duhu
Suverene vladarke organizma
A pokorni neka pomognu
U teškom poslu što nas ima.

Tehnika disanja – naglašava vrač –
Leči sve bolesti! *U mojoj knjizi*
Saznajte o tome kako ćete *dah*
Hvatati uz popust sajamski.

BREATHING TECHNIQUE

Healers have multiplied since the dawn of time
Through epidemics and diseases on the rise
Actual or still unimagined
For which we learn from them the soonest.

This is the start of a favorable time
Of a land that's sold by promises
To presenters of outrageous methods
Of the speediest possible healing.

Mainly they explain the plant
Without any idea how it breathes

Nor do they care what the folk say:
That cure and poison only reside together.

They briskly demonstrate the effect
With a hypothesis of coexistence
Of leaves of grass and human arrogance
That desolates at random.

They preach the psyche in the spirit
Of the organism's sovereign ruler
While, as for the meek, let them help
In this difficult task that has us.

Breathing technique — the soothsayer emphasizes —
Can cure every illness! *In my book*
You'll learn how to catch your breath
With a special discount for the market.

Nadasve divlji origano obavezno!
Oprez! Samo u prepoznatljivim
Bočicama firme Melem komerc!
Krema protiv svraba dolazi gratis.

Brinite o sebi. Rešenja su nadohvat
Ruke na tastaturi. Jedan klik otvara
Svet nesaznat. Na tacni dat da svako
Razume bez čitanja film poučan.

Pisanje reklama nikada nije bilo
Tako jednostavno kao u doba
Vizeulnih animacija fantastično
Složenih i pogoršanog zdravlja.

First and foremost wild oregano, for sure!
But careful! Only in the easy-to-spot
Jars from our company, *Salve Commerce*!
The anti-itch cream comes for free.

Follow self-care. Solutions are as near
As your hand on the keyboard. One click opens
An unknown world. Everyone will easily
Understand the informative film — no need to read.

Writing advertisements has never been
So simple as in the era
Of fantastically complex visual
Animations and of worsened health.

HOLLY BUSINESS

psalam

za Ester

Smiluj se, pogledaj na me.
Dosta si me mučio ljubavlju,
Tamničio me poezijom nedužnu,
Lepotom duše umalo dokrajčio,
Smiluj se, pogledaj na me.

Daj mi da budem estradna zvezda!
Udeli komad celofanskog neba.
Bar jedan CD, jedan spot,
Intervju na jahti sa mnom podari.

Učiniću sve sto želiš,
Izlaziti u susret u zamenu
Za kuću daleko od sveta da se smirim,
Za bazen da povedem život zdrav,
I ja, ropkinja, sluškinje da imam,
Milosti, milosti daj mi!
Uželeh se novih cipela.

Biću ti odana, Tebi i Tvojima.
BUDA, ALAH, KARMA, OM,
SPIRITUS MUNDI, KABALA, AMEN!

Neka me vide s biznismenima i princezama,
Neka me vide na koktelima i trkama konja,
Neka i mene vide!

HOLLY BUSINESS

a psalm
for Esther

Have mercy, take a look at me.
Thou hast tortured me enough with love,
Imprisoned innocent me with poetry,
Almost finished me off with a beautiful soul,
Have mercy, take a look at me,

Let me be a star of the stage!
Share a piece of cellophane heaven.
At least one CD, one video spot,
Grant me an interview on a yacht with me.

I'll do everything Thou wishest,
I'll submit to Thee in exchange
For a house far from the crowd to be at peace,
For a swimming pool to lead a healthy life,
And for me, a slave, to have maidservants,
Mercy, give me mercy!
I do so wish for some new shoes.

I'll be devoted, to Thee and Thine.
BUDDHA, ALLAH, KARMA, OM,
SPIRITUS MUNDI, KABALLAH, AMEN!

Let me be seen with businessmen and princesses,
Let me be seen at cocktail receptions and horse races,
Let me be seen too!

Neka narod govori *Ona kaže,*
Neka jednom pomisle da i ja
Menjam tokove istorije,
Trunku privida promene pošalji
I biću Ti stalno nova.

Osuših se od ozbiljnosti i časti,
Dosta si me mučio.
U limuzini uvedi me u nepregledno
Carstvo Tvoje zabave.
Neka me Tvoji doktori ulepšaju, vrate mladost.
Neka me sveštenice Tvoje odenu u šare od kože otrovnica.
Plave kose željna sam!
Daj mi učitelja joge, masera,
Baštovana sa kojim ću spavati kao sve Tvoje miljenice.
Učini da oživim na posterima,
Da stanem među palme nasmejana,
Kud kročim da Svetom zemljom nazovu
Stopu moju
Daj mi!

Biću ti odana, Tebi i Tvojima,
BUDA, ALAH, KARMA, OM,
SPIRITUS MUNDI, KABALA, AMEN!

Pusti da moje brakove izučavaju
Na fakultetima deca kojoj ionako nema pomoći.
Svaku moju reč da slušaju, sve dok čuju
Niko Te ne može tužiti da ugrožavaš spas.
Nadeni mi ime lako za pamćenje.
Neka svima pripadnem, preklinjem Te!
Iz tamnice nežnosti me izbavi,

Let the nation say *She says*,
Let them think for once that I too
Am changing the courses of history,
Send a sliver of the semblance of change
And I'll be ever new to Thee.

I'm dried out from seriousness and false virtue,
Thou hast tormented me enough.
Take me in a limousine into the impenetrable
Kingdom of Thy amusement.
Let Thy doctors make me prettier, return my youth.
Let Thy priestesses clothe me in motley of poison serpentskin.
I'm yearning to have blond hair!
Give me a yoga teacher, a masseur,
A gardener I'll sleep with, like all Thy favorites.
Make it so that I come to life on posters,
That I stand smiling among palm trees,
Where I tread, let them call it the Holy Land
Give me
My footstep!

I shall be devoted, to Thee and Thine,
BUDDHA, ALLAH, KARMA, OM,
SPIRITUS MUNDI, KABALLAH, AMEN!

Let my marriages be studied
At college by children who are helpless nevertheless.
Let them hear my every word, as long as they hear
No one may accuse Thee of threatening salvation.
Put a name on me that's easy to remember.
Let me belong to everyone, I beseech Thee!
Save me from the dungeon of tenderness,

Od ovisništva savesti spasi,
Veštinu pozornice podari.
Ne mogu više, ne mogu
Da budem samo svoja!

I slaviću Te, Tebe i Tvoje,
Moliću se vitka i gipka,
Krstiću se, padati ničice,
Ljubiti kad god ustreba
Decu iz sirotišta, političare, kamene temeljce
I grobove koje proglasiš svetim.

Biću samo Tvoja
Kad svačijom me stvoriš.

Nećeš se pokajati.
Vapajem se zaklinjem
Svuda ću govoriti da si Ti najbolji producent.
Isplatiću se.
A Ti samo
Dok još me ima, pogledaj na me!

BUDA, ALAH, KARMA, OM,
SPIRITUS MUNDI, KABALA, AMEN!

Save me from dependency on conscience,
Give me the gift of skill on stage.
I can't any more, I can't
Be my own alone!

And I'll glorify Thee, Thee and Thine,
I'll pray, slender and flexible,
I'll cross myself, I'll fall down prone,
Kiss whenever necessary
Children from the orphanage, politicians, the stone foundations
And the tombs Thou declarest sacred.

I'll be only Thine
If you create me everyone's.

You won't regret it.
With longing I swear
I'll say everywhere that Thou art the very best producer.
I'll pay off.
And Thou only
While I'm still here, take a look at me!

BUDDHA, ALLAH, KARMA, OM,
SPIRITUS MUNDI, KABALLAH, AMEN!

DOBA NEŽNOSTI

Otkako postoje
umetnost pisanja
i umetnost čitanja
proveravaju jedna drugu.

THE ERA OF TENDERNESS

As long as they have existed
the art of writing
and the art of reading
have verified each other.

OTVORENO IZA PONOĆI

Milici Dragojlović

Rekle smo: *Ima da imamo kafanu!*
Jednoga dana otvoriće se zasluženo
Vrata »Svitanja« u spomen na »Zoru«
Koju smo mi zatvorile umesto kelnerica
Iz Borče ljubazno odloženog fajronta.

Osvetićemo sve odjednom!
»Poslednji prevoz«, »Otkaz«, »Bivša kladionica«
Ili »Proširene vene« – plemeniti su naslovi
Ako utisak nadživi sadržaj.
Bina u ćošku polutamna kao vino,
Drvene stolice, prave, sa jednom nogom
Kraćom kao u pisca brodskog dnevnika.

Srušen četvrti zid
Obavezno poštovanje pravila
»Koliko sveta, toliko mesta«,
Ćušnuta iza šanka tabla »od-do«
I samo ukrasne brave, zaslužile smo
Katance razvenčane od ključeva.

Slobodno
Kod nas će pevati ko ume
Pevajući ma šta da zapeva
O pustoj želji sopstvene pesme.
Pevači su publika. Trema nas je napustila
Još onda kada su teme pravile gužvu u redovima

OPEN AFTER MIDNIGHT

To Milica Dragojlović

We girls said: *We have to have a café of our own!*
One day they'll open the long-deserved doors
Of "The Crack of Dawn" in memory of "Dawn,"
Which we closed instead of the waitresses
From the city outskirts with the courteously postponed last call.

We'll take revenge on everything at once!
"The Last Bus," "Fired," "Used to Be a Betting Window"
Or "Varicose Veins" — they're noble titles
If the impression outlives their contents.
A podium in a corner half-dark as wine,
Wooden chairs, proper ones, with one leg
Too short, like a ship-log writer's.

A broken fourth wall
Obligatory honoring of the rule
"As many guests, that many places,"
A sign reading "open from- to-" kicked behind the bar
And only decorative locks, we deserve
Padlocks divorced from keys.

At our place
Whoever can will be free to sing
Humming whatever they have to sing
About the empty desire of their own song.
Singers are an audience. We lost our stage fright
Back when sensitive topics caused crowding in the lines

Za iseljeničke vize. Intonacije se javljaju iz daleka,
Sve ređe. Mere opreza si ukinula
Lično prošavši kroz staklo.

Nikad više, milo moje – zapevala si uživo
U studiju državnog Radija, iako je
Ulicama mirno tekla revolucija.
Prošla si u restoranu za poslovne ljude
Kroz tišinu malih zalogaja i dremež
Krotkih kolena pod kodeksom bele maramice
Igrala na stolu *Tri metera somota.*
Nikada nisi imala toliko para
Kao tada u grudnjaku tuge
Dovedene do pucanja glasa
Kafanske pevačice u službi
Poziva stroge vedrine. Nikad više.

Daleko za nama je usmereno obrazovanje.
Dug put od saopštenja komisije za prijem
Novih kadrova: Žao nam je do odelenja
Bolesti duše prošle smo
Isuviše da bismo pamtile
Uz Što *te nema,* što *te nema*
Sa visokom ocenom: Vrlo dobar bol.

U duetu gutale terapiju u boji
Krišom pospešujući sastav pivom,
Dok su naši vršnjaci zdravih živaca
U manjini bežali u klubove zatvorenog tipa
Gde muzika je deo ambijenta
Prijatnog nedogađanja.

For emigrant visas. Intonations send news from a distance,
Ever more rarely. You ended the measures of caution
By personally walking through the glass.

Never again, my dear one — you sang live
In the State Radio studio, even as
Revolution was flowing peacefully through the streets.
You passed through a restaurant for business people
Through the silence of snacks and drowsiness
With meek knees under a codex of white handkerchief
You played on the table *Three meters of velvet.*
You've never had so much cash
As then in your bra of sorrow
Brought to the point of a breaking voice
Of the café singer in service
Of the call of strict cheerfulness. Never again.

The new education is aimed far behind us.
Long the road from the message of the acceptance commission
For new personnel: "We regret to say" that we passed into
The department of illness of the soul
Too greatly to be able to recall it all
To the tune of *Why aren't you here, why aren't you here*
With a high score: Excellent pain.

As a duet we swallowed therapy in color
Secretly rushing the accompanists with beer,
While our peers with the healthy nerves
Fled in the minority to the closed kind of clubs
Where music's part of the atmosphere
Of happy nothing happening.

Bila je zima, »Zora« davno ugašena,
Nedolično obučene ušle smo u kafić
»Šta ima?«, odbile da poručimo više
Puta pogledali su nas sablažnjeno
Bogata deca i strani investitori,
Kao da smo se dogovarale, mada
Nemoguće je po dogovoru otpevati
Do kraja, bez mikrofona, sa dušom
Samo: *Jedna mladost, jedan svjet nade,*
Drugi za te ovaj svjet grade,
Možda na me čeka neki bolji svjet.

Skinule se gole i istrčale van
Uplakane, padale od smeha
Ushićene repertoarom
Uličnih rešenja.

It was winter, "Dawn" was long extinguished,
We went inappropriately dressed to the café
"What's There?", refused to order more
Times they looked at us temptedly
The rich children and foreign investors,
As if we had agreed on it, although
It's impossible to agree to sing out
To the end, without a microphone, with your soul
Alone: *One youth, one world of hope,*
Others are building that world for you,
Maybe some better world waits for me.

We stripped naked and ran outside
In tears, falling over laughing
Delighted by the repertoire
Of street solutions.

PESNIK

za Mišela Marcana

Čudo je to koliko si tu, Mišel.

Čitaju mi se same tvoje pesme,
Pesniče sa Cetinja,
Za čiju su bolest znali svi, tek retki za stihove,
Neizbrisive,
Ona koja ih je, umesto tebe, prevodila tastaturi,
Onaj kome je bila čast da objavljuje tvoje knjige,
Svo troje sahranjeni istoga dana
Na groblju koje ima samo tri kapele.

Naučio si pesmu s najmanjim brojem reči,
Iako ti to nije bila namera. Nestvarno
Prirodan, svoj, duša od čoveka, kako o tebi
I dan-danas govori bolničko osoblje.
Naučio si da voliš i one koji te napustiše.

Okupilo ih je tvoje izmučeno telo
Činom sahrane
Zauvek.
Sin te je ponovo zavoleo. Majka zagrlila
Odbeglu snaju s ogromnim fetusom kajanja
Razumevanjem kakvo ima samo mučenica
Kao izraslinu koje nije svesna.

THE POET

to Mišel Marcano

It's a miracle how much you're here, Michel.

Your poems keep reading themselves to me,
Poet from Cetinje,
About whose illness everyone knew, but few about the verses,
Indelible,
She who, in your stead, conveyed them to the keyboard,
He whose honor it was to publish your books,
All three of you buried the same day
In a graveyard that has but three chapels.

You learned a poem with the fewest words,
Though that was not your intention. Unreally
Natural, your own, such a dear man, as to this very day
The hospital staff says about you.
You learned to love even the ones who abandoned you.

Your tormented body gathered them
With the act of a burial
Forever.
Your son came to love you again. Your mother hugged
Her runaway daughter-in-law with the huge fetus of repentance
With understanding such as only a martyr has
Like a tumor of which she isn't conscious.

Bio si mlad, pred tobom nije bio život.
Bio si lekcija o životu.
Sirot, a potpisan njeguškim pršutom i kačkavaljem.
Na svako moje: „Što si se trošio?! Ovo je luksuz!"
Ti, čija je svaka grimasa bolela, odgovarao si
Smeškom: „Muči, jadna, neka ti kuća zamiriše!"

Vidim tvoj osmeh, Mišel,
Iako se nikada nismo videli
I nikako da te pitam ko ti je dao ime.

Povremeno se čujem sa zajedničkom nam Sanjom:
Najlepše si živ u našim pričama!
Kakva osećajnost – pomislim potom
– otići, a ostaviti sânju
Kao znak
Da ti je i dalje stalo.

Čudo si, neukidivi!
Ništa ti nisi planirao,
A sve je ispalo kako bi hteo
Da si tako zalazan i ozaren
Novim danom na kamenoj terasi
Razmišljao o svojim željama.

You were young, you had no whole life before you.
You were a lecture on life.
Poor, but signed with Njeguši prosciutto and kačkavalj cheese.
Whenever I said, "How could you spend so much!? This is luxury!"
You, whose every grimace was pain, would answer
Smiling, "Shush, poor thing, may your house be fragrant!"

I see your smile, Michel,
Although we never saw each other
And there's no way I can ask you who gave you the name.

Sometimes I hear from our mutual Sanja:
You're the most beautifully alive in our stories!
What sensitivity — I'll think afterwards
— to go away, but to leave dreaming
As a sign
That you have gone on caring.

You're a miracle, uninterruptible!
You didn't plan anything,
But everything turned out as you would have wanted
If you, so in decline and lit
By the new day's sun on the stone terrace,
Had pondered over your own desires.

POGLED

Delile smo sobu:
Ona je noć i dan ležala
Na leđima i s pogledima
Ili na televizor, ili na zaboravljeni
Visoki dimnjak od cigle čiji je dim
Davno rasprodat na tenderu.

Kako izdržava da 10 godina gleda taj dimnjak?!
Kako zabole reči koje prijatelj ispusti neuviđavno
Zaboravljajući da ih prećuti.

Ulazila sam u našu sobu
Da je presvučem, nahranim, napojim
Kafom i vodom i pomognem da puši.
Da prilegnem i poletim sa jatima
Kada se s večeri vraćaju grupno poput dečje ekskurzije
U botaničku baštu da spavaju, ujutro skupa uzleću.

I kuda ovo vodi?!
Obrušila se na moj premor doktorka
Ugledavši pepeljaru, cigarete bez filtera,
Paket muštikli usled koga je njen glas
Dosegao maksimalnu visinu.

Kuda?
Ispustih reč sasvim lagano
Nemajući u vidu, zapravo,
Niti jednog sagovornika.

VIEW

We shared a room:
She lay there day and night
On her back and with views
Either of the television, or of a forgotten
Tall brick chimney whose smoke
Was long ago sold at auction.

How can she stand 10 years looking at that chimney?
How it hurt when my friend let those words out,
Forgetting to keep them quiet.

I would go into our room
To change her diapers, feed her, give her a drink
Of coffee and water and help her have a smoke.
To lie down a bit and fly off with the flocks
When in the evening they return in a group like children from a field trip
To the botanical garden to sleep, in the morning they fly up together.

And where does this lead to?!
The doctor crashed down on my exhaustion
When she saw the ashtray, the unfiltered cigarettes,
The pack of cigarette holders after which her voice
Would reach its maximum volume.

Where to?
I let the words out quite easily
Without having, in fact,
Any single interlocutor in mind.

POVRATAK

Iz mojih koračanja
Rutom svakodnevlja
Nestala je samoća.

U rođenom kraju
Neko me je odžepario
Postah sagovornik neznanom glasu:

Pa šta te još za ovo ovde veže
Gde tvojih odavno nema
A svaka šuša bar jednu lipu sreže

Da zaposedne ulicu hacijendom,
Da parkira svoju lađu,
Il' tek da naruga se vrtu bednom?

Zar tu si da bi oplakivala piljevinu?
Da pomalo skapavaš s gramatičkim greškama?
Zar tu si umesto bivšeg hora da tuliš tugovanku?

Tako me iz dana u dan
Kinji glas dana
Nepozvan, nasilan.

I bivam sve više dete
Iz sopstvenog života negdašnjeg
Zaigrano sred ničije zemlje.

THE RETURN

From my strides
Along the route of everyday
Aloneness disappeared.

In my own neighborhood
Someone picked my pocket
I became an interlocutor with an unknown voice:

Well what is it that ties you to all this here
Where for a long time you've had no one of your own
While every drought brings down at least one linden

To occupy the street with a hacienda,
To moor their boat,
Or else just cuss at the poor garden?

Are you really here to mourn for sawdust?
To die a bit along with the grammatical mistakes?
Are you really here in place of the former choir to extend a dirge?

Thus from day to day
The day's voice bullies me
Uninvited, forced.

And I am more and more the child
From my own life once upon a time
Playing amid no-man's-land.

Preskačem zamišljene paralele lastiša,
Radujem se školicama kojih više nema,
Kradem posečene trešnje iz dvorištâ.

Pričam s počivšim prijateljima
Nikada prisutnijim
U emigraciji smeha.

Noć na zemlji mi nemo poručuje:
I ovo je život, i ovo si ti.
I tvoja je ta senka na goleti.

I jump across imagined parallels of rubber bands,
I rejoice at hopscotch games that are no longer there,
I steal the cut-down cherries from the courtyards.

I chat with friends who are at rest
Never more present
In the emigration of laughter.

Night on the land gives me mute advice:
This too is life, and this is you.
And that shadow on the bare ground is yours.

PREDAJA GRADA

Ja imam strah za ovaj grad.

Od pada ulica u nagađanja
O podzemnim rabotama,
Od izliva psihotičnog otpada
Pod mostom sto se baca u reku,
Od depresije uličnih svetiljki
Od zastarelih obećanja novih vlasti,
Od jutarnjeg kolapsa koji je večernji,
Od prevoznog sredstva
Počivšeg u upotrebi,

Od Zamora materijala
Od divlje gradnje odnosa
Sa pokradenim delovima
Na trošnim temeljima ljubavi.

Imam strah
Od mirenja sa životom u minusu
Od ishoda
Potere gladnih usta na usta,
Od nakota nadmenih mehurova
Iz plastične utrobe vladarke ukusa,
Od paradigme uzornog građanina,
Od svakog izostalog Dobar dan,
Od sopstvenog glasa
Obogaćenog psovkama i drugim ispadima
Osnovnih namirnica bez zemlje porekla.

SURRENDER OF THE CITY

I have fear for this city.

From streets that fall into guessing
About underground intrigues,
From the outpouring of psychotic junk
Under the bridge that jumps into the river,
From the streetlights' depression
From the worn-out promises of new authorities,
From the morning traffic jam that is the evening's,
From the means of transport
That retire while still in use,

From the Fatigue of material
From the illegal construction of relationships
With stolen parts
On ramshackle foundations of love.

I have fear
From settling with life in the red.
From the outcome
Of the loss of hungry mouth-to-mouth,
From the litter of arrogant blisters
From the plastic womb of the empress of taste,
From the paradigm of the model citizen,
From every neglected Good Day,
From my own voice
Enriched with swear words and other sallies
Of basic foodstuffs lacking a land of origin.

Ja imam strah za ovaj grad
Otkako je ljubav otišla na dalek oporavak
A o njoj nasumične izveštaje pišu
Generalne sekretarice generalnih direktora
Iz podneblja sve više egzotičnih,
Otkako ne znam kada smo požurili da starimo
U jednoj godini sustižući tri
Srušili se u davno prošlo
Vreme susreta neotkazanih.

Zid naš ostao sam
Pridržava bicikl boje korozije
Pamćenja obroka na klupi za dvoje
I mape dodira sa čitko ucrtanim osmesima
Slučajnog prolaznika koga šeta pas.

Od nežnosti nepovratne i tako skupe
Ja imam strah za ovu glad.

Ja imam ljubav za ovaj grad
I kada nisam sigurna da postojim
U njegovim parkovima
Naučila sam da hodam, govorim, progutam reč
Predaja sa ljutim nadevima značenja,
Grad drevne demokratije ljubavi
U tvojim i mojim drvoredima
Naučila sam da se poljubac ne uči
I sve uistinu živo jednom biva
Kako ga već ne bi bilo
Nigde van strogog centra:

I have fear for this city
Ever since love left for a distant convalescence
And the general secretaries of general directors
Write random reports about it
From ever more exotic climes,
Ever since I don't know when we've rushed to get old
Managing three years in one
We keeled over into the long past
Time of uncanceled encounters.

Our wall remained alone
It supports a corrosion-colored bicycle
Recollections of a meal on a bench for two
And the map of touches with legibly sketched-in smiles
From a chance passerby whose dog takes him for a walk.

From tenderness unrequited and so costly
I have fear for this hunger.

I have love for this city
Even when I'm not sure I exist
In its parks
I learned to walk, to talk, I gulp down the word
Surrender with the hot topping of significance,
City of the ancient democracy of love
In your avenues and mine
I learned that a kiss can't be learned
And everything truly comes to life only once
So that it can no longer be
Anywhere outside the strict center:

Trougla između Nebojše kule, rimskog bunara i pruskog sata
Gde sam se samo tu predala
Rečnim travama i zvezdanom roblju
Kada najlepše nisam postojala
Osim u zajedničkom jeziku
Imam ljubav za ovaj grad.

Ja imam ljubav u ovom gradu
Skloništa za goli zivot od poverenja
I svoj lift prestupa davnog
Otisak totalnog
Prelaska u drugog i nazad
U pasažu
Obeleženom grafitima onomatopeja
Jecanjem u sebi napuštenog
Kamiona veličine ulice ako se oduzmu
Našeg tela imuna na strah od sprovoda
Komunalnog zakona.

Imam bezuslovnu ljubav za pravila
Izostala
O nepropisnom parkiranju kraj zaborava.

Ja volim ovaj grad nad zonama,
Njegove čuvare bunovnih koraka sa povodcem
Oko ručnog zgloba umesto časovnika,
Grad neprevodivog humora
Iz čijih travnjaka, slivnika, raskopina
Svaki čas ustaje Lazar-devojka
Iz solarnog predaha Silvije Plat,
Sa nebeskog harema spušta se Danica

The triangle of Nebojša Tower, the Roman Well and Prussian Clock
Where only here I surrendered
To river grasses and starry slavery
When I most beautifully did not exist
Except in a common language
I have love for this city.

I have love in this city
Of refuge for trusted bare life
And one's elevator of a long-ago transgression
The imprint of total
Passing into another and back
In the underpass
Marked with graffiti of onomatopoeia
By inward sobbing of the abandoned
Truck as big as the street if you take away
Our body immune to fear from the obsequies
Of common law.

I have unconditional love for the rules
Neglected
In illegal parking next to oblivion.

I love this city above zones,
Its watchmen's dazed steps with a leash
Around their wrists in place of watches,
City of untranslatable humor
From whose grassy spaces, drains, ditches
The Lazarus-girl emerges every moment
From Sylvia Plath's solar pause,
The Morning Star comes down from the heavenly harem

Nad kartama, ulaznicama, propusnicama,
Nakratko se podsmehne ložama za ugledne
Novograđane.

Ona čistom lepotom predaje
Vožnju slepog putnika celom
Narodu na splavu porinutom
Ljubeći
Onaj zid srećom neugledan,

Mig svetiljke,
Sve što dovoljno voli da nadživi.

I taj bicikl, kažem, iz sasvim lične istorije.

Above charts, entry tickets, passes,
Briefly has a smile at the VIP loggias for honored
New-minted citizens.

With pure beauty she teaches
A blind traveler to drive the whole
People on a launched raft
Kissing
That wall unnoticed by luck,

The wink of a lamp,
Everything that loves enough to survive.

And that bicycle, I say, from an entirely personal history.

PUT SVILE

Naili

».. . *a fabula nestaje čim se more pojavi.*«
Danijel Dragojević, »*Uzao*«

Malo-pomalo postajemo privrženi svom kraju
Na način na koji se za ljude vezuju psi i ostali
Ljubimci, ne znajući niti željni saznanja
O meri pripadanja.
Tako je i u našem krugu trafika, rupa na pločniku,
Polupraznih frizerskih salona, ljubaznih apoteka gde
Ostavljamo najviše para, ulubljenih kontejnera,
Izložbenih parkinga i ciganskih zaprega, tezgi
Opremljenih svim što čoveku uistinu treba,
Piljara što nas snabdevaju nostalgijom drznemo li se
Da nekuda otputujemo, u krugu boja, glasova, ponosa
Nas starosedelaca jer samo nama je poznat čas pada
Trošne fasade, konačno odustajanje balkona u doba
Mahom visećih spontano.
Ne umišljamo, već zaista nismo živi ako se uzajamno
Ne pitamo svakoga dana ispred prodavnice »Sinteza«
Kako smo, da li se dete napokon zaposlilo, kako mama
Podnosi ove ludačke promene vremena, kako ih nije
Sramota da onako lupetaju u skupštini, da li ste čuli
Da je deterdžent jeftiniji u drugoj samoposluzi, da,
Ali ko će do tamo da ide, ovde je bliže, a ionako
Sve manje trošimo nas četvoro, češće dvoje, dve,
Ja sama sa mačkom više i ne osećam
Dinar gore ili dole. Na isto izađe.
Nema nama spasa – smejemo se izduženi

SILK ROAD

To Naila

"...the plot is gone as soon as the sea appears"
Danijel Dragojević, "The Hawser"

To Naila

"... the plot is gone as soon as the sea appears"
Danijel Dragojević, "The Hawser"

Little by little we grow fond of our neighborhood
The way dogs and others, favorites, get attached
To people, not knowing nor desiring to know
About the degree of belonging.
So in our circle too there are newsstands, potholes,
Half-empty hairdressers, gracious drugstores where
We leave the most money, battered dumpsters,
Exhibition parking lots and gypsy teams, counters
Fitted out with all a person really needs,
Grocers who'll supply us with homesickness if we dare
Travel away anywhere, in a circle of colors, voices, the pride
We old natives feel, for only we know the hour of the fall
Of a ramshackle façade, a balcony's final refusal at a time
When they're mostly hanging spontaneously.
We don't make it up, no we're really not alive if we don't
Reciprocally ask every day in front of the "Synthesis" shop
How we're doing, did the child finally get a job, how is mama
Tolerating these crazy changes in the weather, how is it they
Aren't ashamed to blab that way in parliament, have you heard
That detergent's cheaper in the other market, yes,
But who can be bothered walking there, here it's closer, and anyway
We four spend less and less, more often we two, mixed or same gender,
It's just me and my cat and I don't feel it any more
If the dinar goes up or down. It comes out the same.
There's no hope for us — we laugh stretched long

Kao da nas neko kroz čašu posmatra sa kesama
Ruke dodiruju tlo, one na noge već sasvim liče poput parova
U brakovima dugim kada dvoje nerazdvojne sestre postanu.
Lagano pletena prisnost komšijskih niti zavodi
Jednakost svakodnevlja i neobičnih priča.
Recimo, juče smo, tačno znam na kom ćošku,
Slušali o Kini, njenom putu svile ka vodećoj sili sveta
Utemeljenoj glinenim vojnicima cara-ujedinitelja Ćina,
Njih 6000 sa naređenjem da svaki ima svoj lik,
O umeću vladanja, dakle, uz uslov različitosti
Naučila sam pošavši po dnevne novine, mleko,
Trešnje tri puta skuplje od kineskih
Nisam okusila niti je moguće
Ništa lepše od generala sa sopstvenim likom
Predaje poklona na ulici, ćošku upamćenom
Po bliskosti koja ide tako daleko
Gde ni misao ne dopire kao gest
Odabira
U prodavnici suvenira.

As if seen through a glass of water with our plastic bags
Our arms reach the ground, they look just like legs like couples
Married a long time when the two become inseparable sisters.
The easily woven intimacy of neighborly fibers seduces
An equivalence of everydayness and unusual stories.
For instance yesterday we heard, I know on just which corner,
About China, its silk road toward ruling power in the world
Founded on the terra cotta warriors of Chin the emperor-uniter,
6000 of them with the order that each have his own face,
Thus, under the condition of distinctness, I learned about knowing
How to rule, having gone to get the daily paper, milk,
Cherries three times pricier than the Chinese ones
I didn't taste nor is it possible
Anything more beautiful than the generals with individual faces
Passing on a gift on the street, the recollected corner
With a closeness that goes so far away
Where not even thought penetrates as a gesture
Of selecting
In a souvenir shop.

ŠEN

Đelem, đelem, lungome dromeja,
Mala dilem, čorore Romesa . . .

Kad vidiš da gledam u nebo
Gospodine
Ne pitaj me da li se molim.
Pusti da budem za sebe
Čudo za tebe i sam
Na istom nebu videćeš:

Glava zna da se odvoji za ljubav pogleda.
Korak uči da utekne od besa ludog
Vozila sa moćnom nostalgijom
Konjske snage.

Moj bicikl poželi da makar jednom točkom
Dodirne visinu gde umesto upravljanlja
Sve teče mirno vazdušnim rekama.
Vidi, niz ruke mi cure oblaci!

Nisi moj gazda, gospodine sa puno para,
Ništa ti ne pripada kao ni meni ova raga
Osim tog dana samo tvog kada stvor
Umesto u semafor put neba
Uspne pogled smiren,
Kao ja koji nikada nisam sticao već tražio
Svoj dom a pitaju me da li se molim.

DIVINITY

Djelem, djelem, lungome dromeja,
Mala dilem, chorore Romesa . . .

When you see I'm looking at the sky
Oh Lord
Don't ask me if I'm praying.
Let me be for myself
A miracle for you and you yourself
Will see in that same heaven:

The head can be lost for love of a look.
A step teaches escape from the rage of a crazy
Vehicle with the powerful nostalgia
Of horsepower.

My bicycle wishes that at least one wheel
Touched the height where instead of management
Everything flows calmly in airy rivers.
See, the clouds are dripping down my arm!

You aren't my boss, mister with all the cash,
Nothing belongs to you just as this raga isn't mine
Besides that day only yours when a creature
Instead of a sky-bound semaphore
Climbs up with a calm look,
As I who never arrived but sought
My house and they ask me if I'm praying.

Pevam i smejem se i plačem kada mi se dete rađa,
I ko će znati zašto sam tužan kada me kiša miluje,
I kuće se kupaju i zemljica pije,
A ja bazam i naletim na odbačeni kišobran!
Samo tada mi se plače valjda.

U njemu vidim vernog slugu
Za hir bahatog gospodara
Skončalog u slomljenoj žici.
Krpu vidim od pokušaja košujle da leti.
Točak se sam do mene dokotrlja i šta ću,
Moram da zaplačem. Dirne me
Sve što voli da živi!
Žena mi kaže da sam poludeo i da bi bilo bolje
Žicu po žicu da kalemim
Za pedale da iskoristim što sam našao
Da ne kukam nego da stvorim
Antenu da se deca raduju.

Kad ostanem živ i dođem kući i sednem i ja da gledam
Nešto da me razgali,
Bože, šta se sve nađe u toj kutiji!
Dok sam skupljao grane za ogrev
I stari hleb da ga prepečemo i ženi našao
Haljine i deci patike i novi dušek neraspakovan
Ni sam nisam verovao.
Nebo pitao gde to ima osim u ovoj državi
Na televiziji a možda i stvarno
Jedni da ručaju u vazduhu, drugi gladni na zemlji?
Dotle se ono punilo ovim dušama iz kutije
U kojoj moja deca gledaju čaure i spljoštene
Konjske snage.

I sing and laugh and cry when my child is born,
And who knows why I'm sad when the rain caresses me,
And the houses bathe and the soil drinks,
While I roam and run into a thrown-away umbrella!
Only then do I likely cry.

In it I see the faithful servant
Of the caprice of a brave lord
Who perished in a broken rib.
I see the rag from a shirt's attempt to fly.
A wheel rolls over to me itself and what can I do,
I have to start crying. Everything
That loves to live touches me!
The wife tells me I'm nuts and it would be better
To bend it wire by wire
On the pedals to use what I have found
Not to fuss but to create
An antenna so the children can be glad.

When I remain alive and come home and I too sit down to watch
Something to put me in good humor,
Oh God, what all can you find in that box!
While I was gathering branches for the stove
And old bread to toast and found the wife
Dresses and sneakers for the children and a new bed still wrapped up
I didn't believe it either.
I asked heaven where you could find it except in this state
On television and perhaps in real life too
Some who lunch in the air, others hungry on the ground?
Until it was filled up with these souls from the box
In which my children watch shells and compressed
Horsepower.

Ćuti nebo.
Ne valjaju ovi zvučnici, tandrču,
Ništa se ne razume.
Slika se kvari svaki čas,
Izem ti kolor crveno-beli!
Kontejner je livada u proleće
U odnosu na ovo smeće!

Gospode,
Ti koji si majstor svetla,
Da li si ikada brojao
Koliko hranjivih boja ima
U da prostiš ostacima?

Keep quiet heaven.
These speakers are no good, they buzz,
Nothing can be understood.
The picture goes bad every moment,
I'll make your color red-and-white!
A dumpster is a meadow in spring
Compared to this garbage!

Oh Lord,
You who are a master craftsman of light,
Have you ever counted
How many nourishing colors there are
In, forgive the expression, the leavings?

SEZONA DOBRIH LJUDI

Kažem ti

ljudi se povremeno sete
      da bi voleli da žive:
      okite jelku,
      zapevaju pesmu koju su godinama
odlagali uz višak uspomena,
      poprave slavinu,
      napišu pismo,
      presade biljku koja začudo
još pruža znake života,
      pomaze podočnjake i reše
da učine nešto za svoj ten.

I muž ženu izvede na piće,
i ćerka majku u park,
i sin uspori hod na putu s posla i osmehne se
vremenu kada je oca zvao tata.

Dobri su ljudi.
Koliko mogu
      i uz pomoć prilika.
Ako samo obratiš pažnju primetićeš
ima ih još koji bi i Boga da poštede
      mučnih ispovesti.
Ima ih koji redovno hrane kučiće
      i napuštene stvorove uopšte
pažnjom.

THE SEASON OF GOOD PEOPLE

I tell you

people sometimes remember
        that they would love to live:
        decorate a Christmas tree,
        sing a song that for years
they postponed with an excess of memories,
        fix the faucet,
        write a letter,
        repot a plant that miraculously
still gives signs of life,
        rub cream on their dark circles and decide
to do something for their skin tone.

And a husband takes a wife out for a drink,
and a daughter takes a mother to the park,
and a son slows his pace coming from work and smiles
at the time when he called his father Daddy.

People are good.
As much as they can be
        and with help from circumstances.
If you just pay attention you'll notice
there are still those who would like to spare even God
        from ugly confessions.
There are those who regularly feed stray dogs
        and neglected creatures in general
with attention.

Postoje ljudi koji umeju
        da daju
        a da nas ne povrede
požrtvovanjem.
Ima ih koji i bez davanja pružaju.
Koji postoje
        privatno
u ovim javnim vremenima.

Dobri su ljudi. Ipak se vole
        bar na određeno vreme.
U nekim ulicama koje potom pamte,
uz drvo koje poštuju jedninom,
priljubljeni uza zid
        koji u ličnim istorijama nije
srušen zbog nove gradnje.
I sete se dodira u nevreme,
opišu ponovo svaki zabranjeni pokret
        precizno, krišom, ispod stola
        na nekom sastanku,
i čak zažale što su godinama marljivo radili
        na sticanju odgovornosti
        i zazirali
        od lepote pada.
Ima ih još koji se postide.
Ima ih čiji stid opstaje u slozi
        s praznikom življenja.
Hrabri su ljudi.
        Sve dok vole
arhitekturu uzajamnih htenja.

U ovom danu
divljenja vredni

People exist who know how
        to give
        without offending us
with their sacrifice.
There are those who offer even without giving.
Who exist
        privately
in these public times.

People are good. They still love each other
        at least part-time.
In some streets that they remember later,
by a tree that they respect with the singular,
pressed up against a wall
        which in personal histories is never
knocked down for a new building.
And they remember the touch at the wrong time,
they describe anew every forbidden movement
        precisely, secretly, under the table
        at some meeting,
and they even regret that they worked diligently for years
        at acquiring responsibilities
        and shied away
        from the beauty of falling.
There are those who feel ashamed.
There are those whose shame arises in harmony
        with the holiday of living.
People are brave.
        As long as they love
the architecture of shared desire.

In this day
worthy of wonder

čak i oni sa belegom,
        i kada ga skrivaju rukavom,
        i kosom preko čela.

Pa i ti i ja
        s grešnom rešenošću da svoje postojanje
        pretvorimo
        u strogost lišavanja,
        u zgađenosti nad kolotečinom,
svetim svakodnevljem,
        u savršeni san
        o moru
od kojeg svaka luka postaje jalova.

Ti i ja i ta ljubav
zbog koje svaka druga ljubav
        ostaje nevoljena.
Ti i ja i ta pomama
        za trajanjem.
Ti i ja
        suviše
ti i ja.

Ali biva
da jutro samo od sebe
        u dobroti osvane,
i vatricu plamen tihovanja primi,
i umine ta napast prožimanja
brže
nego što to usavršeni
        u nestrpljenju
        ti i ja
        javljamo preko i-mejla.

even the ones with a mark,
>even when they hide it with a sleeve,
>and with hair swept over the forehead.

And you and I too
>with sinful decisiveness that we shall turn
>our existence
>into a severity of deprivation,
>into disgust over the routine,
the sacred everyday,
>into a perfect dream
>of the sea
from which each harbor grows sterile.

You and I and that love
for which every other love
>remains unloved.
You and I and that lust
>for duration.
You and I
>too much
you and I.

But it can happen
that morning all by itself
>dawns in kindness,
and takes on the little fire the flame of quietude,
and soothes that obsession of being filled
more swiftly
than that perfected
>in impatience
>you and I
>communicate over e-mail.

SKADAR

Pravili smo dete od peska.
Pesak je nastao od kamena.
Kamen ne postoji bez mora.
U mašti začeta
neophodnost roditelja
nema uzor.

Noć je opšte mesto.
Dan oboleo od zidanja.
Jednom započeta, zidanica se nastavila
u obrušavanju.
Samo je naša ljubav mogla da izađe na kraj
s pitanjem uporišta.

Pesak je pohrlio pesku.
Postali smo
od sna o stvaranju
nedeljiva imenica.

Baš kao ova barka ili boca ili zatureni ključ,
kao ispušteni glas žene koji grabi
mladunče u trku,
uvek drugačiji zalazak sunca,
uvek drugačiji izlazak sunca,
mi smo
usvojenici pejzaža
i zrno ponosa
Majstora Promene.

SKADAR

We made a child of sand.
The sand arose from stone.
Stone can't exist without the sea.
The necessity of a parent
conceived in imagination
has no pattern.

Night is a common place.
Day sickened from building.
Once begun, the construction went
on in knocking down.
Only our love could manage
with the question of a foothold.

Sand rushed at the sand.
We originated
from a dream of minting
indivisible nouns.

Just like this barge or bottle or misplaced key,
like the voice let out by a woman who grabs
her cub at a run,
always a different sunset,
always a different sunrise,
we are
the landscape's foundlings
and a grain of pride
of the Master Craftsman of Change.

LIMENKA

Pisala sam pesme ljubavne
U prošlom vremenu
Kao i sva književnost.

Svaka je stala u povod
Prilagođenog sećanja
Na neupamćeno.

Varale su kao i sve ljubavne
Podatne slike jakih ritmova, žudnja
Odzvanjala kao testament.

Volele se međusobno
Nastrane kao fotografije
Što jedna drugu ne vide.
U pozadini leta
Belo grožđe i laka odeća
Naspram sunca prozirne kose.

Ti, ljubavi, svoja, besramna,
I nasmejani starac navikao na strance,
U jednoj ruci drži štap, drugom stiska

Limenku koka kole, njom te grli
Na mene polaže pogled siguran
Da razumem prizor, a nisam –

Stvarno je samo
Prvi i poslednji put.
Bez brige.

SODA CAN

I wrote love poems
In the past tense
Just like all literature.

Each one arose in connection
With adapted recollection
Of the unremembered.

They cheated just like all the amorous
Supple images of strong rhythms, longing
Rang out like a testament.

The poems loved one another
Weird like photographs
That don't see each other.
In the summer background
White grapes and light clothing
Towards the sun of translucent hair.

You, love, so unusual, shameless,
And a smiling old man used to foreigners,
In one hand he holds a cane, with the other he squeezes

A can of coca-cola, he puts that arm around you,
He lays his gaze upon me certain
That I understand the sight, but I didn't —

What's real is only
The first and last time.
No worries.

Mudra starina, od života zna –
Svi smo ionako turisti.
A baš sam te mnogo volela.

Noćas bih mogla pisati pesme još tužnije
O teškim grozdovima, tankim majicama,
Tvojim džepovima punim školjki,

O svemu što se ne vidi na tom snimku,
Što se na prvi pogled daje
U sebi ovekovečeno.

Uzalud su mi kasnije naklonjeni pričali
Kako ta klupa na autobuskoj stanici –
Čiča i ti, nasmejani kružite Internetom.

Glup je napor trećega
Da drugom saopšti
Ni u prvom te nema!

Volela sam te, jer zašto bih bila
Na čitav svet ljubomorna
Što te i on u ekranu gleda?

Ništa sada nemam sa tim.
Ni tuga mi nije ostala,
Kao što neko sačuva autobusku kartu.

Ko zna kad, u kom vremenu,
Oko je izoštrilo želju,
Uspomena učinila *klik!*

Wise old man, he knows it from life —
We're all tourists anyway.
But I really loved you a lot.

Tonight I could write poems even sadder
About heavy grapes, thin t-shirts,
Your pockets full of shells,

About everything invisible in that snapshot,
That gives itself at first glance
Recorded for eternity in itself.

In vain did the ones who were so inclined tell me later
How that bench at the bus station —
The old guy and you, laughing, were surfing the Internet.

It's stupid for a third to make the effort
To inform the second one
You aren't even in the first one!

I loved you, for why would I be
Jealous of the whole world
That it too sees you on the screen?

I have nothing to do with that now.
Not even the sadness stayed with me,
The way someone might save a bus ticket.

Who knows when, at what time,
The eye focused its desire,
And memory went *click*!

SOMETIMES I FEEL LIKE A MOTHERLESS CHILD

Moja prva prekinuta ljubavi,
Muzo čežnje. Ti život si
Još jednog izostalog filma
Kamernog, niskobudžetnog.

Moja Euridika, robinja Kerberovog carstva,
Zbog koje sam nastanjena u ulici Banović Strahinje
Jer ti prolasci su duži i od košmarnih snova
Koliko traju obilazak i povratak iz smrti.

Kadrovi su zbrkani i snažni
Kao i ostaci ispovesti sa nalazišta Lidija:
On mi ne da da je viđam, svoju ćerku.
A tako sam htela da studiram minerale.
Čula sam da liči na mene. Ili me teše?
Bila sam dete, on pedofil! Sipaj!
Da, volela bih da vidim tvog psa.
Ne brini, samo su kolena odrana,
Zagrlila sam drvo da ne bih pala.

Beži pod hitno! Oblači se usput! Dolazi gazda!
A on je javna/moćna ličnost,
Tamanitelj maloletnika. Nema dalje.
I ovo što znaš je previše. Lud je!
Kada već moram da se prikazujem kao pratilja,
Želim tebe da zadržim. Ne dam te.
Ma, posle ćeš o Persefoni, nestani!

SOMETIMES I FEEL LIKE A MOTHERLESS CHILD

My first interrupted love,
Muse of longing. The life you are
Of one more leftover movie —
Art-house, low-budget.

My Eurydice, slave of the realm of Cerberus,
For whom I came to be in the street of Banović Strahinja
Because I've passed through even longer than in nightmares
So long lasts the turn and return from death.

The shots are jumbled and powerful
Just like the remnants of confession from the site of Lydia:
He doesn't let me see her, my daughter.
And I so wanted to study minerals.
I've heard she resembles me. Or are they comforting me?
I was a child, he the pedophile. Pour me one!
Yes, I would like to see your dog.
Don't worry, just that my knees are skinned,
I hugged a tree so that I wouldn't fall.

Run away now! Get dressed as you run! The boss is coming!
And he is a public/powerful figure,
An exterminator of the underaged. No way to go on.
What you know is already too much. He's nuts!
If I already have to cover for him, act the chaperone,
I want to keep you. I won't let you go.
Fine, talk about Persephone later, lay off!

Prelepa si – šapućem na stubištu.
Ti si moja poslednja slast –
Čujem kako se reči udaljavaju –
Ja padam.
Hvala ti što me pratiš tako daleko,
Divoto, ljubavi – mislim da je rekla i to.

Gde je? Kako ne znate? Pa, nije isparila?!
U bolnici, ali je molila da ti ne kažemo kojoj.
Kolege iz redakcije vodiča kroz Beograd
Odjednom su nežni ljudi, budući preplašeni.

Ludim.
Nađem je.
Ime, tačnije. Ne pamtim kako
Nadigravam javnu/moćnu ličnost, tamničara.
Evo, pitala sam je – uzbudila se bolničarka
Premda sama u smeni.
Ne želi da je vidite. Voli Vas. Samo prenosim reči.
Ali ne odustajem. I nađem te, čitavu jednu
Večnost kasnije, u čituljama.

Sada sam starija od tebe, Lidija.
Ne zato što smo iz istoga kraja, ma gde
Otišla, vraćam se ulicom Strahinjića Bana.
Gledam se sa balkonom, nasmejem se
Mogućoj asocijaciji na Juliju. Nikako!
Ali ko je, zapravo, Strahinja? Ti ili ja?

Ostala si u analima mojih usana, dlanova, pupka.
Uživala si u mestima gde sam te svuda vodila.
Za razliku od mnogih Hađana, tvoje je lice čitko

You're so beautiful — I whisper on the stairs.
You are my final delight —
I hear the words move far away —
I'm falling.
Thank you for accompanying me so far,
My wonder, my love — I think she said that too.

Where is she? What, you don't know? She can't have evaporated!?
In the hospital, but she begged us not to tell you which one.
The colleagues who edit a guide through Belgrade
Are suddenly gentle people, being frightened.

I'm raving.
I find her.
Her name, that is. I don't recall how
I outsmart the public/powerful figure, the jailer.
Here, I asked her — the nurse got excited
Although alone on duty.
She doesn't want you to see her. She loves you. I'm just passing on her words.
But I don't give up. And I find you, one entire
Eternity later, in the obituaries.

Now I am older than you, Lydia.
Not because we shared the same neighborhood, wherever
I go away to, I return by the street of Strahinjić Ban.
I watch myself on the balcony, I laugh
At the possible association with Juliet. No way!
But who, in fact, is Strahinja? You or I?

You've remained in the annals of my lips, palms, my navel.
You took pleasure in the places where I took you everywhere.
Unlike many citizens of Hades, your face legible

Poput crno-bele fotografije
U dnevnom listu
U oglasima
Za one za kojima žale
Poneki bližnji,
Epitel,
Nepotpisano
Groblje abortiranih reči.

Like a black and white photograph
In the daily paper
In the announcements
For those who are mourned
By some near and dear ones,
The epithelium,
The unsigned
Graveyard of aborted words.

DUH IZ PLINSKE BOCE

Vidi, tata! Veeelika pomarandža! Tek prohodala
Pliva sunce tatino! Morem obasjan belutak vajan
Poverenjem. Sva je kako treba! San roditelja.
Oči njegove plave. Osmeh bonaci nalik. Uvojci od zlata.
Šta priča? Da li to govore opasne avanture šumske i brodske
Pred ulazak u san ili uistinu nešto vreba njegovu mezimicu?
Nema vremena za pitanja u svetu prenaseljenom prevratima
Nestalo je utočište za odgovore.

Do maločas zamajan kulom od peska prestravljen
U vodu skače ne gleda već grabi šakama roditelja
Što naglo izrastaju u opasnosti. Ne stiže da primeti
Naočari na dno prispele niti mari za ishod bliskog
Susreta s nemani. *Izlazi napolje!* Uspeva da vikne
Premda dah hvata jedva zlim slutnjama napadnut
Vidi ono čega nema. Najstrašnije budući nepoznato.

Veeelika narandžasta riba! Kliče radosna ona
Čije vaspitanje zadato vrlim precima zabranjuje
Strah. Psovke su ružne. Mržnja vređa. Voleti treba
Unapred. Pogotovu kad ne razumeš. Pruža ručicu
Da tati pokaže to što kraj nje pluta. Ili na pučini?

Iako namah obnevideo on je tu da razazna bocu
Plinsku i u njoj zarobljen gas porinut ko zna kad.
On mora znati da je misao bilo koja lakša od vode
Stoga ka obali mira plove teške vesti o drugoj strani
Odakle pristižu iznemogli od gladi ili duše ispuštene
Iz tela kojima se morski živalj hrani. Klobuk nesvarljivog
Pred pucanjem je nežni želudac Mediterana.

THE SPIRIT FROM THE GAS BOTTLE

Daddy, see! A biiiiig orange! Daddy's little sunshine has just learned
To walk and is floating! A bright white sea-lit pebble
Sculpted by trust. Infused with a fortitude of heaven! A parent's dream.
With his blue eyes. A smile serene as dead calm. Curls of gold.
What's she saying? Is a dangerous forest-and-boat adventure speaking
As before sleep, or is something truly threatening his pet?
There's no time for questions, in a world packed with overthrows
The sanctuary for answers has disappeared.

All dedicated until just now to a sand tower he leaps
Horrified into the water, doesn't look but scoops with a parent's hands
That suddenly grow in case of danger. He has no time to notice
His glasses, sunk to the bottom, nor to dread the outcome of a close
Encounter with some monster. *Get out of the water!* He manages to yell
Though breath barely suffices, beset by evil misgivings
He sees what doesn't exist. Most frightening being what's unknown.

A biiiiig orange fishy! joyfully shouts the girl
Whose upbringing imposed by worthy forebears forbids
Fear. Dirty words are ugly. Hate harmful. You must love
In advance. Especially when you don't understand. Her little hand
Points to show daddy what's floating by her. Or some leagues to sea?

Though suddenly deprived of sight, he's here to discern a gas
Bottle and inside it captive vapor, launched who knows when.
He must know that any thought is lighter than water.
Toward the world's shore therefore floats heavy news of another country
Which those exhausted from hunger come from, or souls released
From bodies the marine population feeds on. The Mediterranean's
Tender digestive tract is a bubble of the indigestible before a shooting.

On je tu da nanjuši pokoreni vazduh afrički
Brani ako treba svoje mladunče od ostataka oca
Utopljenog u nadi da umakao je pogromu u toku.
Što dalje dete skloniti od boce koja odašilje
Krike oslobođene iz koliba od pruća i blata
Urlike vojnika uvek neprijateljskih šapat
Krijumčara duša u barkama izgriženim rđom
Šum zamaha noža pirata i tupi udarac sa mesta
Gde vrh bodeža dočekuje kost.

Otac je tu da vidi oca koji se moli za spas voljenih
Dok šakama roditelja grabi ka boljoj obali preklinje
Dah da ga ne izda a bocu da ga odnese što dalje tamo
Gde svakako više je sreće nego u domu sada bivšem.

Šta je to, tata?! Vrišti dete izniklo u srećnoj porodici
U kojoj pomno odmeravaju se tonovi i nepoželjna
Oštra gesta zatire. Gde su prethodni kako kažu deci
Davno prognali sramnu laž kolika god da je cena
Onoga što zaista jeste.

Prazna boca, sine! Nije ništa. Istinu prenosi uplašenoj kćeri.
Ništa više i nije ta prazna boca plinska nesaznatom dramom
Trajno zaptivena. Prećutano neka ne sazna. Ili što kasnije.
Ceo život je pred njom za savete o poželjnom izbegavanju
Plodova Mediterana riba školjki rakova trava zanjihanih
Vremenom u kojem su i oni postali ljudožderi.

Previše prilika za užas saznanja o potomcima graditelja
Piramida okovima pohranjenim u morima koja predano
Vežu pustoline sa žarkim zemljama plodne muzike
Ropskih duša. Jednom pitaće ona recimo o hip hopu.
I tata će morati da objasni bluz od najgoreg početka.

He's here to sniff out the vanquished African air,
To defend his offspring if need be from the remnants of a father
Who drowned in hopes of escaping a pogrom in progress.
To move the child as far as he can from the bottle that emits
Cries freed from a cradle of twigs and mud,
The howls of always enemy soldiers, the whisper
Of smugglers of souls in boats gnawed by rust,
The noise of a pirate's knifestroke and the dull blow from the spot
Where the dagger's tip meets bone.

The father's here to see a father praying for his loved ones' rescue
While with a parent's hands he scoops to beseech a better shore
That breath not forsake him, that the bottle carry him off as far as possible
To where there is surely more luck than in his home, now former.

Wat's dat, daddy? shrieks the child, who sprouted in a happy family
In which they carefully weigh vocal tones and any undesirable
Sharp gesture is rooted out. Where as they tell the children predecessors
Long ago grubbed up shameful untruth, however high the cost
Of that which truly is.

An empty bottle, honey! Nothing. He conveys truth to his startled daughter.
And that empty bottle of gas is indeed nothing more, sealed lastingly
By unknown drama. Stay: let her not learn what's kept quiet. Or not till later.
She has her whole life before her to get advice about desirably avoiding
The fruits of the Mediterranean fish shells crabs seaweeds swaying
In a time when they too became swallowers of people.

Too many chances for horror learning about the heirs of those who built
The pyramids, fetters deposited in seas that faithfully
Link wastelands with the torrid lands of slave souls'
Fertile music. One day she'll ask about hip-hop, let's say.
And daddy will have to explain the blues from their worst beginning.

Bar još malo neka pošteđena upoznaje oblike
Zvezda korala njihanje trava mreža i jedara
Simetriju potpuno istovetnih žena pogleda izdubljenog
Pod crnim maramama nanizanih na klupama kraj obale.
Neka što kasnije iskusi zaludnost čekanja kojim more
Kao i svaka ljubav života vernošću čežnje uzvraća.

I miris masline da mrzi što duže zlato tatino prelepo
Daleko od slasti gorkih ukusa koji zrelošću opčine
Čula neizostavno tako da ništa drugo ne osete
Do čari bola. Vinsku pitkost nostalgije.

Ništa od toga neka ne bude sada
Na ovom letovanju
Čitavih godinu dana
Planiranom samo za njih dvoje.

At least a little longer protected, let her recognize the forms
Of stars corals swaying seaweed nets and sails
The symmetry of completely identical women with fixed gazes
Under black kerchiefs, strung along benches by the shore.
Let her taste as late as possible the futile waiting with which the sea
Like any other love in life faithfully responds to longing.

And as long as possible let her hate the scent of olive, daddy's pretty girl
Far from the sweet of bitter tastes that with ripeness unavoidably
Spellbind the senses so that they perceive nothing other
Than the charms of pain. That winy drinkable nostalgia.

Let there be none of that now
On this summer vacation
Planned all year long
For just the two of them.

TAKT

Čitavog leta
U vreme debate o vrelini kao znaku
Početka ili poodmaklog kraja sveta
On je krečio.

Otkrivao zidove belim
Rečima sušio fleke
Zanesen i precizan
U odlaganju grubosti vanjskih.

Zgrada naspram zgrade.
Naši stanovi se gledaju.
Zapleti klize niz fasade.
Nema straha od dodira.

Majica s njegovog prozora
Upija ritam mog prostora.
Obratno jednako zvuči
Uporednom prepuštanju.

Pouzdan hvat valjka
Tek tu i tamo blag
Upad četke u pogled
Prijanja od prekoputa.

Bez mogućnosti nijanse
I ljubavne interpretacije
Betonska prostudušnost
Ćuti sopstveno usijanje.

TACT

All summer long
In a time of debate over the heat as a sign
Of the beginning or the advancing end of the world
He was painting.

He revealed the walls with whitewash
Dried the spots with words
Enthusiastic and precise
Putting off the rudenesses of outside.

Building across from building.
Our apartments face each other.
Plots slide down their façades.
There is no fear of touching.

The t-shirt from his window
Imbibes the rhythm of my space.
The inverse sounds equal
To a parallel indulgence.

A dependable grip of the roller
Only here and there mild
The brush's leap into view
Of adherence from across the way.

Without any possible nuance
Or amorous interpretation
Concrete indifference
Keeps quiet its own incandescence.

ULIČARKE

O, strasti
Prema zdravoj hrani izvesnosti!

Ti – svaki, Morao si ih bar jednom
Videti za života bez obzira
Promašenom ili tebi vrednom.

Mitomanijo raskrinkana, obožavam te!
Parodijo porekla:
Braćo i sestre začeti ispod mostova i na travnim
Površinama,
Mili moji preci iz žbunova!
Sa čičkovima međ maljama!
(I vi iz fotelja uspešnih preduzeća,
I vi od fetusa navikli na limuzine,
Iz bliske davnine – moji vi!)

Posledice najslađeg stiska
U istoriji neznamenitog zida!
Sorto anonimna,
Čitave Troje
Ljubavne sluzi!

Hvala ti nauko, saučesnice,
Na svakom četvrtom DNK
Iz uličnog koktela!
Ljubim ti svaku utičnicu, fajl, kap

STREETWALKERS

O, passion
For the health food of certainty!

You — every one,
You must have seen them
At least once in your life regardless
Missed or valuable to you.
Demystified mythomania, I adore you!

The parody of origin:
Brothers and sisters conceived under bridges and on grassy
Surfaces,
My dear forebears from the bushes!
With burrs among your locks!

(And you from the armchairs of successful enterprises,
And you accustomed to limousines since you were a fetus,
From the nearby olden days — you, mine!)

Results of the sweetest pressure
In the history of an unfamous wall!
Anonymous breed,
Whole Troys
Of the mucus of love!

Praise to you science, accomplice,
On every fourth DNA
From the street cocktail!
I kiss your every outlet, file, drop

Uzajamnog otkrića!
Nepoznata, proširena porodico,
Prošlosti bez rama, slavim te!

Moj ženski rode,
Od sloge zimnica i gumica u boji.

Čuvarke mraka i reda
Tu su da poštuju:
Koja, za koga, kada, koliko, šta.
One su ozbiljne.
Život je u pitanju.
Treća smena.

Sa plastičnom torbicom i puknutom čarapom
Uslužile su više mušterija
Od kasirke-udarnice iz megamarketa.
Nema te države, pola, organa,
Automobila sa tamnim staklima ili bicikla,
Nesrećnih brakova i usklađenih zajednica,
Radnika, policajaca, učiteljica,
Teške muke nevinosti,
Ne postoji otrov skrivanog ukusa
Kojem nisu izašle u susret.

Pouzdane,
Nežno u uho ili nožem preko lica zamoljene,
Smesta
Odlažu vaše intime u ponor barskog toaleta,
Zauvek i uz garanciju strogo
Poverljivog vodovoda.

Of one more
Epochal discovery!
Unfamiliar, expanded family,
A past without frames, I celebrate you!

My feminine gender,
Winter stock of harmony and colored rubberbands.

Guardians of dark and order
They are here to respect:
Which one, for whom, when, how much, what.
They're serious.
It's life in question.
The night shift.

With a plastic purse and a run stocking
They have served more customers
Than the hero-of-labor cashier at the megamarket.
There's no state, sex, organ,
Automobile with tinted windows or bicycle,
Unhappy marriages and harmonious units,
Workers, police, teachers,
Agony of male virginity,
There exists no poison of hidden taste
That they haven't done their best for.

Dependable,
Requested gently in the ear or with a knife across the face,
On the spot
They send your intimacies off into the abyss of the bar's toilet,
Forever and with the guarantee of strictly
Confidential sewage.

Čvrsta kao viteška čast
Minulih vremena
Njihova je reč:
Nema ljubavi.
Strogo bez emocija, jezika, posetnice.
Nismo se nikada sreli – jasno!
Po obavljenom poslu – ćao!
Grohot po narudžbini, a dotle
Bez smeha!
Zbog izostale erekcije,
Alergije na prezervativ – dešava se,
Previše se dešava, stoga
Bez stenjanja: *To, samo tako, mama!*

Bez pritužbi, reklamacija, primisli
Na telefonski poziv, drugo viđenje.
Bez ljudskih prava za nesebično
Razumevanje humane svrhe.

Same
Poput konjanika iz narodne pesme,
Bez zaštite, često namerno,
Kako bi krišom rodile vas.

O, vi, usvojenici,
Sa belegom od jeftinog ruža,
Razmažena deco
Sopstvenih avantura!
Vi, braćo po nemanju
Pojma.

Firm as the knightly honor
Of bygone times
Their word is:
There's no love.
Strictly without emotion, tongue, visiting card.
We've never met — clearly!
Once the job's complete — so long!
Roaring when ordered, but until then
No laughter!
Because of a lacking erection,
An allergy to condoms — it happens,
Too many happen, therefore
Without moaning: *That, just like that, mama!*

Without any fuss, reclamation, thought
Of a telephone call, another meeting.
Without human rights for an unselfish
Understanding of a humane purpose.

Alone
Like the rider from the folk song,
Without contraception, often on purpose,
So they could give birth secretly to you.

Oh, you, adopted children,
With the mark from a cheap lipstick,
Pampered children
Of your own adventures!
You, brothers in having
No idea.

Kćeri buduća:
Vidiš li me u ordinaciji,
Na krevetu za hitne slučajeve?
Mama ne skida smešak sa plafona!
Zna majka da je u vozu, da nas na kraju
Truckanja i usputnih stanica
Čeka neonski raj!

Devojčice, domaćice, babe,
Službenice, podstanarke, beskućnice,
Tamne i bele pûti, kosooke, plave,
Ćelave, debele, mršavice,
Nepismene, poliglotkinje –
Sestre, ljubavnice, majke!

O, vi bez premca
Prestupnice!

Grešna vam ljubim prečasne skute!
I za večnu ljubav ištem oprost
Neukaljane kćeri.

Future daughter:
See me in the doctor's office,
On the bed for emergency cases?
Your mama doesn't shift her smile off the ceiling!
Mother knows she's in the train, that at the end
Of the jouncing and way stations
A neon paradise awaits us!

Little girls, housewives, grannies,
Office workers, subtenants, homeless women,
Dark and light skinned, cross-eyed, blond,
Bald, fat, skinny ones,
Illiterates, polyglots —
Sisters, lovers, mothers!

Oh, you matchless
Outlaws!

Sinfully I kiss the hem of your garment!
And for eternal love I seek forgiveness
Of your untainted daughter.

STANJE STVARI

Retki su stihovi
dugo je
popunjavanje prostora.

Mrzovoljna
od zaostale želje
da voliš i budeš voljena.

THE STATE OF THINGS

Verses are rare
filling up space
is long, long.

Bad-tempered
from the lagging desire
to love and to be loved.

TAMO DALEKO

majci

Možda je limun zaista žut onoliko
Kilometara koliko putuje svetlost.
Kao što dečaci imaju najveće uši na železničkim postajama.
Devojke se bacaju u more da dočekuju mornare
Samo u određenim kulturama,
U pričama koje su uvek putničke radi
Zalaska sunca u pustinji neko mora da ode
U pustinju po doživljaj.

Daljina ima pravo što postoji.
I snovi neosporivi.
Nema to veze s nostalgijom.

Čežnja se dobija u nasledstvo, pesma jeste
Slepi putnik u genskom kodu.
Deda je voleo »Tamo daleko«, uz vino.
Posle treće čaše ni kvalitet vina nije tema.
Putnika put nauči o važnosti raspoloženja,
Da sa neznancem ćuti prisno.
Deda je znao da je loza ljubavi neispevana.

Da je voljenost tamo gde zamišljamo voljene,
U sličnostima,
U svom liku radi koga, zapravo, valja otići.

THERE FAR AWAY

to my mother

Maybe a lemon truly is yellow
Just as many kilometers as light travels.
The way boys have the biggest ears at railway stations.
Girls throw themselves in the sea to welcome the sailors
Only in particular cultures,
In stories that are always traveling ones for the sake
Of sunset in the desert someone must go away
Into the desert to get the experience.

Distance has the right to exist.
Just like indubitable dreams.
It has nothing to do with homesickness.

Longing's obtained by inheritance, song is
A blind traveler in the gene code.
Grandpa loved *There Far Away*, with some wine on the side.
After glass three the quality of the wine's not a topic either.
The trip teaches the traveler the importance of mood,
To stay intimately quiet with the ignoramus.
Grandpa knew that the grapevine of love is unsung.

That being loved is there where we think of the loved ones,
In likenesses,
In a character of one's own for which, in fact, it's worth departing.

I da nema loše berbe saznao je
Sve što čovek može da zna o pripadanju
Budući stranac.

Ono čemu mislimo da težimo
Dobro je čuvano
Od nas.

And that there's no bad vintage he found out
All that a person can know about belonging
While being a foreigner.

What we think we are tending towards
Is well guarded
From us.

VAJNA TAJNA

Plemeniti poklonici poezije,
Taj uzvišeni soj,
Uglavnom ne slute mnoge pute
Svirepe kud zapada pesnički rod.

I to je pravda lepotom nazvana
Ravnoteže.
Dok nekog boli, drugi da vole verse.
Za to vreme bumerang plete vreže.

U tim ukrštajima
Nikome znanog voznog reda
Zapravo
Nastaju pesme.

Inače
Bog vam ne dao ono što vam pesnik
Ni mahnit ne bi poželeo da spoznate
Te ponore gde niču najlepše reči.

WANNABE SECRET

Gentle partisans of poetry,
That elevated breed,
Principally don't suspect the many brutal
Paths by which the poetic clan strays.

And that's the justice named by the beauty
Of equilibrium.
While one's in pain, another is to love versas.
In that time the boomerang weaves elflocks.

In these crossroads
Of a transit schedule known to no one
In fact
Poems do arise.

Otherwise
God forbid He give you what the poet gives you
Not even a madman would want you to perceive
Those chasms where the loveliest words spring up.

HOD

Šetači koji idu jedan drugom
u susret, ukrštaju poglede.
Tada se novo biće ljubavi
rastavlja na dvoje.

WALK

Walkers who head toward each other
meet at some point, cross glances.
Then a new being of love
separates into two.

APOKALIPSA PO ORFEJU

Čuo sam da mi je nešto ispalo.
Ne napušta me svrab.
Umoran za još jednu noć,
verovatno slep,
rekao bih da me uhode.

Nastojim da se ne okrenem,
da vas ne izneverim budući.
Ko zna šta je Euridika
u stanju da uradi
u stanju kamena.

Koračam na prvi pogled nedužan.
Ako se vrati, ona će nastaviti da odlazi.
Hodom ubijam strah :
tvoj, boga alatki,
njen, boginje oblika,
svoj – pisca slika.

Šta ako nestane pesma?
Šta ako nastupi
smak donjeg sveta?

THE APOCALYPSE ACCORDING TO ORPHEUS

I heard myself drop something.
The itch never leaves me.
Tired out for one more night,
probably blind,
I'd say someone was tailing me.

I force myself not to turn and look back,
not to betray you, creatures of the future.
Who knows what Euridice
is capable of doing
in a state of stone.

I stride at first glance guiltless.
If she comes back, she'll keep on going away.
I kill my fear with walking:
yours, god of tools,
hers, goddess of forms,
my own — writer of images.

What if the poem vanishes?
What if what steps out
is the end of the underworld?

NEW AGE

Kada je majka, baba i prababa Jana
U 92. konačno proglašena neproduktivnom,
Odložili su je u dom za stare i beskorisne,
Deca, unuci i praunuci udruženi
Razume se u najjeftiniji objekat
Te namene gde je osoblje
Neprijatno razdragano
Uselilo tvora kako bi tobože
Razgalilo smorove tu deponovane.

Nema milosti tamo gde nema ljubavi,
A koja je redak prirodni talenat,
I blesavo je tome čuditi se u doba
Brzog hoda, odnosno *power walk*-a,
Koji je samo kršten u Americi.

Nema ljubavi jer sve je pokorio strah
Od neizlečivog virusa siromaštva
(ako ga jednom zakačiš, gotov si)
Za koji nema leka, nema spasa
Osim preventivnog bežanja od zaraženih.

Nema osude, pa tako nikoga da prašta
Novu aplikaciju nagona – preživeti.

Kada je Janina unuka Kerol En
U 42. ostvarila svoj san obrevši se
U beloj kuhinji ličnog vlasništva
Čime je zaokružila opremanje

NEW AGE

When mother, grandmother and great-grandmother Yana
Was finally declared unproductive at 92,
They put her away in a home for the old and useless,
Her children, grandchildren and great-grandchildren united
Of course into the cheapest facility
Of that purpose where the staff,
Unpleasantly exasperated,
Settled a skunk in order supposedly
To dissipate the ennui deposited there.

There's no mercy where there's no love,
And which is a rare natural talent,
And it's silly to marvel at that in a time
Of quick moving, or rather the *power walk*
Which is only christened in America.

There's no love, for everything's overcome by fear
Of the incurable virus of poverty
(if you catch it once, you're through)
For which there's no cure, no salvation
Except preventative fleeing from the infected.

There's no judgment, and so no one to forgive
For the new application of the instinct — to survive.

When Yana's granddaughter Carol Ann
Actualized her dream at 42 acquiring
In the white kitchen of her private property
With which she surrounded the furnishings

Svoga doma koji podseća na NLO,
Stala je, sela tačnije, na trem SVOJE kuće,
Nategla pivo iz flaše i cele noći se čudila
Onome što oseća, što ne oseća tačnije.

Pa, zar nije red da posle tolikog truda
Prekovremenog rada i odricanja
Od ličnih užitaka, budem ako ne srećna,
Onda bar zadovoljna, ispunjena?!

Njena bivša devojka se u vreme dopremanja
Svemirske kuhinje našla takođe sama, smirena
Posle gadnog raskida, uvreda, svađa oko toga
Kome pripadaju trosed, plava vaza i makaze,
Sred drumske prašine Kolorada, zaprepašćena
Lepotom indigo zvezdanog neba kakvo do tada,
Premda nomadske ćudi, videla nije u krovnom prozoru
Svog kadilaka niti u jednoj noćnoj vožnji, a bilo ih je.

Bože, mislila je dok su tamo odakle je krenula
U punom gasu teatralno podižući prašinu,
Unosili hi-tec pećnicu, tri metra frižidera,
Kako sam ikada mogla da pomislim
Da sam očajna, da je ljubav iluzija?
Da nisam volela, da laž su emocije,
Da nema vere u sreću do kraja života,
Ne bi bilo ni izdaje, niti ovog zvezdanog neba,
Pustinje koja oslobađa sva čula poput galopa
Mustanga, projurila bih kroz život,
Ili on kroz mene, ne spoznavši slobodu!

Of her house that resembles a UFO,
She stood up, more exactly sat down, on HER house's porch,
Took a swig from a beer bottle and marveled for nights on end
At what she felt, more exactly what she didn't feel.

For isn't it right that after so much labor
Working overtime and renunciation
Of personal pleasures, I should be if not happy,
Then at least satisfied, fulfilled?!

Her former girlfriend at the time when the space kitchen
Was being prepared was also alone, serene
After the ugly break-up, insults, arguing about
Who owned the three-seat sofa, the blue vase and scissors,
Amid the highway dust of Colorado, staggered
By the beauty of the starry indigo sky which till then,
Though nomadic in nature, she had seen neither in the sunroof
Of her Cadillac nor in one night journey, and she had had a few.

God, she thought while where she had left
At full throttle theatrically raising dust,
They were bringing in the high-tech oven, the three-meter fridge,
How could I ever have had the thought
That I was desperate, that love is an illusion?
If I hadn't loved, if emotions were a lie,
If there were no faith in happiness until life's end,
There would have been neither betrayal nor this starry sky,
A desert that frees all the senses like a mustang
Galloping, I would have raced through life,
Or it through me, without getting to know freedom!

Živela bih jednoličnu sigurnost
Isplanirane američke domaćice,
Po svoj prilici zamrla u beloj ćeliji
Privida doma, šetajući po njoj čašu,
Ne ispuštajući je kao porod šake,
Žal za nečim što ne znam ni šta je,
Histerična, iz dana u dan luđa
Od klopke nedogledne adaptacije,
Od poricanja
Tolikih zatomljenih želja,
Utrnula
Od usamljenosti!

I would have lived the monotonous safety
Of the well-organized American housewife,
In all likelihood have died out in the white cell
Of a phantom house, walking my glass around it,
Not letting go as if it were my fist's infant,
Regret for something that I didn't know what it was,
Hysterical, more crazy from day to day
From the lid of unending adaptation,
From denying
So many smothered wishes,
Gone numb
From loneliness!

ŽIVOT I ZDRAVLJE

Neko se rodi svoj
I to je neizlečivo.
Ona u zemlji koju je snašlo
Da bude opomena poreskim obveznicima
U zemljama neodoljivim za emigrante
O zlu komunizma na kojem počiva
Idila Zapada.

Na toj strani se moralo
Biti nesrećan.
Svaka majka je dojila baksuza.
Očevi su hapsili očeve
U ime socijalne pravde
Jednakosti u alkoholu, seksa kao saradnika
Tajne policije i prava na izbor
Između omče i skoka kroz prozor
Iz nekog razloga uvek zatvorenog.
Ili upravo zbog spektakla pada stakla?

Na toj strani deca su se rađala kao mudraci
U skloništima
Poezije, sporta, zabranjenih ljubavnih balada
O zvezdanim noćima i zvucima tišine
Rizikujući da zbog slike negativnog primera
Iskuse popravni dom
Ili pak odlazak na daleki front gde bi pucala
Ne decu jednako
Osuđenu podelom sveta
Socijalnom pravdom.

LIFE AND HEALTH

Someone's born their own way
And it's incurable.
She in a land where it happened
For her to be a reminder to taxpayers
In lands irresistible for emigrants
Of the evil of communism that rests
Beneath the Idyll of the West.

On that side one had
To be miserable.
Every mother nursed a jinx.
Fathers arrested fathers
In the name of social justice
Of equality in alcohol, sex as a collaborator
With the secret police and of the right to choose
Between the noose and a leap out the window
That was for some reason always closed.
Or precisely due to the spectacle of falling glass?

On that side children were born as sages
In shelters
Of poetry, sport, banned love ballads
About starry nights and the sounds of silence
Risking a taste of reform school
For the image of a negative example
Or else departure for a distant front where they would shoot
At children equally
Condemned by the division of the world
By social justice.

Mala Martina je sama odabrala prezime
Očuha Navratilova čim je izgovorio reči spasa
Bekhend i forhend.
Tako se zvala njena ljubav
I onda kada bi je čitav svet
Nazivao pobedama najbolje teniserke ever
U istoriji
Znala je od malena
Da istinitije od imena
Postoje retki od ljubavi
I svi ostali.

Na drugoj strani, začudo, ništa manje
Usamljenosti onih koji umeju da vole.

Kupila je lični prostor zarad počinka.
Ne Svetinju Izolacije gde se puca na uljeza,
Već kako bi u toj kući na miru volela
Narandžasti zalazak sunca,
San dečjih igrica i bivšu jednu sobu o praznicima,
Tišinu jutra boje leda,
Zelenu travu novog doma svežu
Od povika Indijanaca golih u sedlu
Koji ni mrtvi ne napuštaju svoju zemlju,
Jednu ženu, ako je moguće zauvek
I pse beskućne čiji njuh nepogrešivo
Prati granicu koliko treba kilometara ili milja
Do tla ljubavnog.

Danas je prvi decembar njenog novog života.
Slavi ga usponom na Kilimandžaro
U rečenici: *Hoću da živim, hoću da volim!*

Little Martina herself chose the surname
Of her stepfather Navrátilov the moment he spoke the saving words:
Backhand and forehand.
That's what her love was called
Even when the whole world would call her
The best woman by victories in tennis ever
In history
She knew from an early age
That more genuine than names
There exist the rare ones of love
And then all the rest.

On the other side, for a wonder, no less
Loneliness of those who know how to love.

She bought a personal space for the sake of rest.
Not a Sanctuary of Isolation where they shoot trespassers,
But so in that house she could love in peace
The orange setting of the sun,
The dream of childish games and the former one room on holidays,
The silence of a morning the color of ice,
The green grass of a new home fresh
From the shouts of Indians naked in the saddle
Who even dead don't abandon their land,
One woman, if possible forever
And homeless dogs who unerringly scent
The border of all the kilometers or miles it takes
To reach the ground of love.

Today is the first December of her new life.
She celebrates it by climbing Kilimanjaro
In the sentence, *I want to live, I want to love!*

Da nije teške bolesti, možda, ni sama ne zna,
Niko to ne zna
Može li se uistinu spoznati življenje.
Zdravlje je tajna ove planete
Još pre uranijuma, oslobođenih aditiva
U flašicama za bebe, starija od postanja.

Otuda planinski vrh, možda, ne zna ni sama,
Osim da je suština uspeća
Primanje nagrade pejzaža, spoticanje o kamen, pad, smeh
Krezubog vodiča, novi ukus čaja,
Nežnost u toplim očima životinja koje bez ideala
Jednakosti, pravde ili kapitala
Pružaju najviše mleka i kada je ispaša skromna

U strmoj niziji, tamo gde niko ne poželi golet
Buduće visine niti teži boljem
Gde već je dobro
Bez osvojenog kraja.

That there's no severe illness, perhaps, she herself doesn't know,
No one knows that
Whether they can truly comprehend living.
Health is the secret of this planet
Even before uranium, purified of additives
In bottles for babies, older than genesis.

Thence the mountaintop, perhaps, she doesn't know herself,
Except that the essence of ascending
Is accepting the landscape's prize, tripping on a stone, a fall, the laugh
Of the gap-toothed guide, a new taste of tea,
Tenderness in the warm eyes of animals who without ideals
Of equality, justice or capital
Offer the most milk even when pasture's modest

In the steep valley, there where no one wants the bare rock
Of future heights nor aspires to better
Where it's good already
Without a conquered end.

NOTES

ANESTEZIJA

The first line and the later repetition refers to Izet Sarajlić's poem "Mala velika moja, večeras ćemo za njih voljeti" (My great little one [feminine], this evening we'll love for them), in which the speaker recalls friends who had died in WWII, promising to keep them alive in his thoughts.

BELA

Serbian typically spells foreign words phonetically, so the title here conveys both the Italian *bella* (beautiful) and Serbian *bela* (white).

DANAK

"Danak" primarily means "tribute" or "tax," as in a tax paid "in blood" in the Ottoman Empire, from the time when Serbian and other non-Turkish boys would be taken away and raised to serve in the Ottoman army. Its secondary meaning of "an early part of the day" is important enough in this poem to relegate the more usual meaning to this note.

DNEVNIK SITNIH NEZGODA

In Serbian, the reference to "baj pas" (phonetically, "bypass") recalls the root of *baj*ka (fairy-tale), while *pas* means dog.

FADO

A Portuguese singing tradition, most commonly found in semi-public settings like cafés and restaurants. Frida, in line 7, is of course Frida Kahlo; *mi buen amor* (my good love).

»40 dana nisam napisala pesmu«

In the Orthodox church, special memorials and services are held 40 days after someone's death.

IME REKE
The first name of poet Wisława Szymborska recalls the Wisła, the longest river in Poland, although this poem was written in New York City.

MOJ KRAJ
"Moj kraj" means both "my neighborhood" and "my end." There was no way to keep both meanings — perhaps "my end of the city"?

HOLLY BUSINESS
Esther is the name that singer and performer Madonna (Louise Veronica Ciccone) adopted when she took up study of the Kaballah.

OTVORENO IZA PONOĆI
"Zora" (Dawn) was a famous and beloved *kafana* (café-bar) in an old part of the city of Belgrade that attracted a highly cultured clientele: journalists, actors, writers, etc. The italicized words are titles of well-known traditional songs. The longer quotation ("*Jedna mladost . . .*" is from Croatian popular singer Josipa Lisac's song "O jednoj mladosti" (About a Youth).

PREDAJA GRADA: The repeating line "I have fear for this city" recalls the 1952 poem "Odbrana našeg grada" (Defense of Our City) by Miodrag Pavlović (1928–2014). Nebojša Tower, the so-called Roman well (actually built in the 18th century), and clock are all located in the oldest part of the city, along with the famed park Kalemegdan.

PUT SVILE
The phrase "psi i ostali" / "dogs and others" recalls the novel of that title by Belgrade writer and feminist Biljana Jovanović (1953–1996).

ŠEN
The epigraph comes from Olivera Katarina's recording of the official hymn of the Roma people, which can be translated: "I'm coming, I'm coming

along the long roads,/ I'm meeting beautiful Roma people"; thanks to
<https://lyricstranslate.com/en/djelem-djelem-im-coming-im-coming.
html>.

SKADAR
The title refers to a famous epic song, "The Building of Skadar," which
has a common folk theme. Three brothers are building a city, but a *vila*
(a South Slavic fairy, but more threatening along with her beauty) keeps
destroying what they've built. She finally demands that one of the broth-
ers' wives be walled up in one of the structures; the older wives refuse, but
the youngest wife agrees, asking them to leave her a tiny open window
through which she can nurse her baby.

SOMETIMES I FEEL LIKE A MOTHERLESS CHILD
The African-American spiritual in the title should be familiar to readers.
Strahinja Banović is the hero of yet another epic song: Turks have attacked
the fortress where he lives with his wife and both their families; while
Strahinja is out fighting, one of the Turks falls in love with Strahinja's wife
and kidnaps her. After the fighting ends, Strahinja searches for her every-
where, eventually finding her in a tent with the Turk. The men battle with
swords; Strahinja kills the Turk and asks his wife whether she wants to re-
turn with him. She rides on the horse behind him as they head back to the
fortress. There, everyone, including her parents, condemns Strahinja for
bringing home a whore. This existential loneliness (Strahinja's, his wife's,
or both) is vital to the poem.

TAMO DALEKO
"*Tamo Daleko*" and its translation as "*There Far Away*" are italicized
as titles of a song sung by Serbian soldiers of the First World War — a
favorite, as the poem states, of the poet's grandfather.

BIOS

Marija Knežević was born and grew up in Belgrade. She holds a Bachelor's degree in Comparative Literature and Literary Theory from the University of Belgrade and a Master's degree in Comparative Literature from Michigan State University. Her books include poetry, essays and fiction: *Hrana za pse* (Food for Dogs, 1989), *Elegijski saveti Juliji* (Elegiac Advice to Julia, 1994), *Stvari za ličnu upotrebu* (Things for Personal Use, 1994), *Doba Salome* (The Era of Salome, 1996), *Moje drugo ti* (My Other Thou, 2001), *Querida* (Dear, 2001), *Dvadset pesama o ljubavi i jedna ljubavna* (Twenty Poems on Love and One Love Poem, 2003), *Knjiga o nedostajanju* (The Book of Longing, 2003), *Ekaterini* (2005; translated into English by Will Firth, 2013), *In tactum* (2005), *Uličarke* (Streetwalkers/Strays, 2007), *Knjiga utisaka* (A Book of Impressions, 2008), *Fabula rasa* (2008), *Šen* (Divinity, 2011), *Tehnika disanja* (Breathing Technique, 2015), Auto (2018), and *Krajnje pesme* (Local/Neighborhood Poems, forthcoming), and some selections of her poetry. She has translated, among other things, a book of poems by Charles Simic, *Kasni sat* (A Late Hour, 2000).

Sibelan Forrester teaches Russian language and literature at Swarthmore College in Swarthmore, Pennsylvania. She has published translations of fiction, folktales, poetry, and scholarly prose, including *The Silk, the Shears* by Irena Vrkljan (1999), *American Scream* by Dubravka Oraić Tolić (2005), *The Diving Bell/Воздушный колокол* by Elena Ignatova (2006), *The Russian Folktale* by Vladimir Propp (2012), *What Remains* by Slava Polishchuk (2013), and *The Cataract* by Milica Mićić Dimovska (2016).